Kleine Seiten

PRA

PRAGUE

GREAT CENTERS OF ART

PRAGUE

Edited and with an Introduction by Vladimír Denkstein and Jiří Kotalík

ALLANHELD & SCHRAM
MONTCLAIR

GEORGE PRIOR
LONDON

Translated from Czech
by Vladimír Vařecha

Published in the United States of America in 1979
by Abner Schram Ltd., 36 Park Street, Montclair, N. J. 07042
and Allanheld, Osmun & Co., 19 Brunswick Road,
Montclair, N. J. 07042

Distributed by Universe Books
381 Park Avenue South, New York NY. 10016

Published in the United Kingdom in 1979
by George Prior Associated Publishers Ltd.
37-41 Bedford Row, London WC1R 4JH
ENGLAND
ISBN: 0-86043-280-7

Library of Congress Catalog Card Number: 78-58354
ISBN: 0-8390-0225-4
Printed in the German Democratic Republic

Designed by Horst Erich Wolter

Motif of jacket: Master of the Vyšší Brod Altar.
The Lord's Nativity. Detail

This work is the joint effort of the directors, curators,
and technical staffs of the institutions listed below.
The material was compiled and edited by Vladimír Denkstein and Jiří Kotalík,
with the assistance of Zoroslava Drobná.

Articles:

CONTENTS

An ancient and renowned city in the heart of Europe, Prague was once the center of the historical Kingdom of Bohemia, and is today the capital of Czechoslovakia. In its thousand years of history, enchanted pilgrims from all over the world have paid lavish tribute to this lovely city. Prague is frequently described as the "Art Treasury of Europe," a judgment inspired by the beauty and rarity of its architectural monuments and by the wealth of art treasures of both Czechoslovakian and foreign origin. The extent and quality of its early art treasures reflect the eventful thousand-year history of the country and its leading metropolis.

From her earliest history, Prague's advantageous position in the center of Bohemia made her the focus of life and commerce in central Europe. Converging trade routes allowed the native dynasty of the Přemyslides to unify the country under their rule, and Romanesque Prague was the royal seat and center of the Přemyslide Empire, which played a significant role in European politics in the twelfth and thirteenth centuries.

Guarded by two castles, the legendary Vyšehrad on the right bank and Prague Castle at Hradčany on the left, Prague extends over both sides of the Vltava River. The river valley provides a natural setting for the unique panorama that centuries of creative endeavor have produced. The stone arches of the Judith Bridge, predecessor of the famous Charles Bridge, spanned the river as early as the twelfth century, and the foundations of more than thirty churches and about fifty stone houses built during the reign of the Přemyslides have been preserved in the *Staré Město* (Old Town) to the present day. The stone buildings of Prague, which formed a rich, quasi-urban complex, were unusual in the central Europe of those days, and it was not long—in the middle of the thirteenth century—before Prague became an actual city, by standards of the late Middle Ages, boasting the first perpendiculars of Gothic architecture and the first belt of walls, which enclosed the settlements on both banks of the Vltava.

The rapid growth of Prague reflected the great economic changes that occurred in the thirteenth and fourteenth centuries, particularly the increased mining of Bohemian silver and the development of a money economy based, from 1300, on the minting of the "Prague groschen." Town burghers, a powerful new force in feudal society, were making their contribution to the wealth of the country through both trade and guild manufacture. They also influenced artistic development as the new Gothic style emerged.

The fourteenth century, when Bohemia was ruled by kings of the Luxemburg dynasty, John, Charles IV, and Wenceslas IV, was a period of medieval Prague's greatest economic, political, and cultural development. Charles IV, the most illustrious of the three monarchs, was both King of Bohemia and Holy Roman Emperor. Drawing upon the wealth and power of the Bohemian state, he made Prague one of the most important centers of European politics and trade and at the same time accomplished its magnificent physical transformation. By virtue of its architectural riches and the intensity and high level of its cultural life, Prague had as much importance in central Europe as had Paris and Dijon in the west. It is with Charles IV that the most outstanding ventures in Prague's architecture, culture, and religious life are associated: the founding of Charles University, the raising of the Prague bishopric to an archbishopric, the founding of the *Nové Město* (New Town), the construction of Gothic St. Vitus' Cathedral in the Hradčany Castle, the construction of a new stone bridge, and the erection of the mighty Castle of Karlštejn, not far removed from Prague, as a fitting home for the crown jewels of the Holy Roman Empire, which Charles brought to Bohemia in 1350. During his reign, the widespread building activity also gave the city innumerable churches, chapels, and cloisters, which transformed its silhouette with their upthrust Gothic spires, turrets, and steep roofs and earned Prague the name of "the city of a hundred towers." Prague Castle's roofs, which Charles IV had covered with gold "that they may shine and glitter in clear weather for a long distance," may have given rise to the *epitheton constans* "Golden Town," celebrated two centuries later in panegyrics at the Court of Emperor Rudolph II, and an image associated with Prague to this very day (though more often abroad than inside the country itself).

Under these favorable conditions the Prague of Charles IV and Wenceslas IV became a great center of art. Wood carvers, painters, and artisans in related crafts worked mainly in the town workshops. A collection of their work has been preserved by the Confraternity of St. Luke. In architecture and architectural decoration, the main center was the renowned Parléř's workshop in the vicinity of St. Vitus' Cathedral. Rare evidence of its organization and methods of work may be found in the workshop's well-preserved weekly accounts for the years 1372–1378.

It is impossible to contemplate the collective activities of these workshops without recalling the leading part played by strong, creative personalities, who by their daring and extraordinary gifts marked out a new course of development in the arts. Some left an unmistakable personal mark on their work, even though their names are not known, for example, the Master of Vyšší Brod and the Master of Třeboň, painters, and the sculptor of the Krumlov Madonna, to mention only the best known. Others have been identified, for example, Theodorik, painter, and, most notably, Prague's two leading architects of the second half of the fourteenth century, Matthias of Arras and his successor Petr Parléř, whose works and achievements brought postclassic French Gothic to its logical conclusion and opened the way to new avenues of style. In Gothic painting and sculpture, Prague became the most brilliant star in that splendid creative outburst which characterized the Bohemian School as it was later called by art historians. The number of Bohemian Gothic monuments that have been preserved is imposing; yet this represents only a fragment of the original total.

Charles' complex and contradictory personality, in which traces of an early humanism glimmered through the more traditional medieval piety, was also characterized by a collector's fanaticism. Throughout his life he collected medieval rarities, relics, and curiosities out of profound religious zeal and out of the desire to increase the splendor of his royal throne; but he also had the true collector's mania, the need to collect for the sake of collecting. As Emperor he could easily satisfy this passion, and in time the immense wealth of Charles' treasury grew to more than seven hundred objects, including precious stones and rare works created by goldsmiths, embroiderers, and illuminators. Housed at St. Vitus' Cathedral, it was one of the largest treasuries in Europe and had immense material and incalculable artistic value. Charles himself wrote with pride to Arnošt of Pardubice, Archbishop of Prague, "There can hardly be any city in all Europe (excepting Rome) where the pilgrim would find more relics than in the metropolitan cathedral in Prague."

Our insistence on the importance of Charles IV's acquisitions is not due to their intrinsic worth alone. The St. Vitus treasury also served as an early model in the evolution of the modern museum. In the Middle Ages, kings' treasuries were usually accessible to only a small circle of the elite. The objects in Charles IV's treasury in St. Vitus' Cathedral, however, were exhibited for public worship. The Holy Roman Empire's crown jewels and other precious relics were also exhibited to the public, with the Pope's consent, in a special chapel built for the purpose on the large New Town square. These public displays on certain holy days drew to Prague hosts of pilgrims from all parts of Bohemia and the Empire. They were prompted by Charles' religious sentiments; yet they afforded the general public and not just the King's Court the opportunity to enjoy the rare treasures amassed by the Emperor.

Charles' interest in collecting was carried on by his elder son and successor to the Czech throne, Wenceslas IV (1378–1419). Though not so high-minded a statesman, he did inherit his father's feeling for culture, especially for the fine arts. Witness is a rich set of illuminated books, once part of Wenceslas' library, which are among the supreme exemplars of medieval book illustration in the late fourteenth and early fifteenth centuries. The man-uscripts (most are now in the former Court Library in Vienna) furnish evidence of the cultivated taste of their royal purchaser and of his wide literary outlook. Less bound by religious constraints than his father, Wenceslas combined an interest in the learned works of his day with a manifest delight in the artistry of their illustrations. In this he was certainly close to his contemporary John of Berry, Duke of Burgundy, who is generally regarded as the first grand collector in the period when the Middle Ages were giving way to the modern era.

Tracing the origins and development of any modern European nation is never easy; tracing Czechoslovakia's history is, perhaps, the most complicated task of all. Being the heartland of Europe had drawbacks as well as advantages, for throughout history Prague and all Bohemia (and Moravia and Silesia) were caught in nearly every political and religious current that crossed Europe. After the Přemyslides, the country was governed or exploited by a succession of foreign rulers—Ger-man, Austrian, Hungarian, Polish, Swedish. For a while Prague's star outshone Vienna's as the seat of the Holy Roman Empire, but her dominance did not survive the jockeying for temporal power by the various royal houses, the religious wars, and Czech passion to retain national and cultural iden-tity.

For our purposes it is less important to know Czech history in detail than to understand that the creation, acquisition, preservation—and destruc-tion—of Czechoslovakia's art treasures are inextri-cably linked with that history.

Charles IV (and to a lesser extent Wenceslas IV) gave Prague its golden age, both historically and culturally, but political and religious develop-ments soon turned in a different direction, inflict-ing serious damage on the city's artistic treasures. In 1419, the year of Wenceslas IV's death, the "Warriors of God," inspired by the ideas of the preacher and patriot Jan Hus, began their struggle against the extravagances and abuses of the Roman Church. Stressing a return to early Christian morality and a new and more just order in the world, these precursors of the Reformation precip-itated the Hussite wars which marked the open-ing of two centuries of intermittent civil war. In the early fighting—the Hussite wars alone lasted over fif-teen years—the architectonic face of Prague was severely damaged (late Gothic construction at the close of the fifteenth century compensated only in part for the losses), and in the churches irreplaceable sculptures, paintings, and liturgical articles were also destroyed. Prague Castle, too, was pillaged, not by the Hussites but by undisciplined soldiers serving Charles' own son, Sigismund, who had become King of Hungary by marriage and who had succeeded in taking the throne of Bohemia from his brother.

The turn of Prague's political fortunes again brought the House of Hapsburg to power in 1526, and Prague entered the Renaissance under a Haps-burg sovereign. So gradually did the new Renais-sance styles influence the city's over-all artistic design, however, that it was not until the second half of the sixteenth century, after the Prague Castle fire of 1541, that Renaissance architecture took hold. By this time, the role of builder was shared equally by the Royal Court, the nobility, and the burghers. The extent of these undertakings, con-centrated mainly on secular buildings such as palaces and burghers' houses, increased markedly in the period of the late Renaissance.

In the Prague of Hapsburg Emperor Rudolph II (1576–1612), the quality of the royal art collec-tions improved. Earlier, in the first half of the sixteenth century, the first Hapsburg contribution to the Castle collections was made by the Bohe-mian Regent, Archduke Ferdinand of the Tirol, son of Emperor Ferdinand I, who installed a col-lection of weapons, rare books, and coins in the rebuilt part of Prague Castle. This collection was not destined to stay there long, for as early as 1567, on leaving Prague, the Archduke took it with him to Ambras Castle in the Tirol where it formed the beginning of his subsequently famous collection of art and historical treasures. Thus the Prague period of the Ambras collection was only an overture to subsequent widespread collecting activities of the 9

Hapsburgs, which, on Prague soil, was to culminate in the celebrated *Kunstkammer* (Treasury) of Rudolph's time.

The art-loving Rudolph, the only Hapsburg who elected to make Prague his permanent seat and practically never left it during the thirty years of his reign, put together a splendid collection, made up of thousands of paintings, sculptures, and handicrafts. Art was his life passion, and his interests ranged from the days of antiquity to his own time. His large collection was not merely a royal treasury of assorted riches but a real art gallery, the composition of which was determined by the breadth and level of Rudolph's tastes as collector and the influence of the contemporary school of Mannerism.

Rudolph's art collection and the diversity of his cultural and intellectual activities were not isolated in a courtly enclave, as is generally thought. Rudolph had a particularly lively interest in the art of his own day and was not only a collector, but also an ardent and generous patron, attracting to his Court eminent artists from northern and southern Europe, who met there and produced new works of sculpture, painting, graphic art, and handicrafts. The Court of Rudolph II thus became a major center of European culture and a focal point of late Renaissance art, which, in the spirit of Mannerism, combined beautiful form with philosophical meaning. The engraving of the interior of Vladislaus Hall by Jiljí Sadeler suggests the busy traffic and bustling activity of the market place in Prague Castle where collectors and art lovers from all over Europe congregated.

Rudolph also amassed curios characteristic of Renaissance cabinets. The Emperor's interests, particularly in the last eccentric years of his life, included alchemy and astrology, which in point of fact—thanks to the work of Tycho de Brahe and Johannes Kepler—made the Prague Royal Court the cradle of modern astronomy. The exacting demand of the collector for exceptional works of craftsmanship was met partly by imports, but more significantly through the specialized and mature craft of Prague's own workshops. It was on Prague soil that the splendid globe dedicated to Emperor Rudolph and other handsomely designed astronomical instruments were produced. Kašpar Lehman's work during his stay in Prague and experiments in engraving rock crystal in the Prague glassworks were applied to glass technology, and had a major impact on the rapid development of the renowned Bohemian glass. Jewelers, goldsmiths, armorers, and other craftsmen also reached a high level of design and production.

The work of Prague's artisans was not for the Emperor alone, but was eagerly sought by the local nobility and wealthy merchants. Stimulated by the example of the Court, these two forces in Renaissance society pressed their cultural claims, thus precipitating a growing demand for luxury articles that were formerly the exclusive preserve of the Court. In doing so, they laid the groundwork for the first private libraries and private collections of art. Thus the relationship between Prague and the Court was mutually rewarding, the city taking an active part in producing the art to satisfy Rudolph's passion for collecting while at the same time absorbing stimuli for its own cultural development from the lively cultural scene at the Castle.

After the death of its founder, Rudolph's magnificent collection had a complex and sorry history, which has been clarified only recently thanks to the painstaking artistic and historical analysis undertaken by Professor Jaromír Neumann who successfully traced what remained of the collection in Prague and in other great galleries and museums of the world. The ravages of war, predatory raids by armies aimed at previously selected works of art, changes in the royal seat of the Hapsburgs, and the transfer of works of art to other centers of the Austrian monarchy, together, accounted for the dispersion of this finely integrated collection. The Prague Castle collection was so decimated and the gallery so badly damaged that they had to be completely rebuilt in the second half of the seventeenth century to meet the needs of the emperor of that day.

As the late Renaissance passed into the Baroque period, the further development of Prague culture was suddenly checked by the uprising of the predominantly Czech and Protestant Estates in 1618, which initiated the protracted European conflict known as the Thirty Years War. The defeat of the revolt in the Battle of White Mountain in 1620 is a fateful landmark in both the political and cultural history of the country. Bohemia, Moravia, and Silesia lost their independence for the next three hundred years. Incorporated into the multinational Austrian

Catholic monarchy, they were gradually subjected to the centralist absolutism of the Vienna government and exposed to religious and national oppression. At the same time the victorious Counter Reformation broke existing links between Czech art and Dutch art and opened the way to a new style brought into the country by artists from Italy and Catholic countries in the southern part of the Austrian Empire.

In Bohemia, Baroque art was first associated with the country's oppressors, and it took a whole century for the new style to take root and become assimilated with creative Czech forces. In time, the blend of native and foreign matured into the supreme expression, which, in the early eighteenth century, enriched the development of art throughout Europe with its high artistic values and genuinely individualistic forms of representation.

It was in Prague that these changes were reflected most clearly. Though Prague ceased to be a royal seat, the city, as the center of a defeated country, was the site for widespread construction by powerful families of the nobility who had grown rich through confiscations. Among those who shared in this boom were nobles who had come with the conquerors from abroad as well as those among the country's own aristocracy who had sided with the victors and who, in return for remaining faithful to the Hapsburg throne, earned the Emperor's favor.

The monumental new palaces devoured the city's rambling old residential quarters with the same recklessness as the huge building complexes of the Jesuit colleges, which were the focal points of the Counter Reformation and the centers from which the effort to recatholicize the city and the whole country was directed. It was in the most important of these, the Clementinum in the Old Town—to which the catholicized Charles University became attached—that an important center of Baroque culture developed. Here, too, the foundation was laid for the large and valuable University Library, to which the first collections devoted to natural science and astronomy and open to the public were attached in the course of the eighteenth century.

The power of the high nobility was reflected not only in the monumental scale of the early Baroque palaces and the magnificence of their outer façades but also by the glittering social life and the display of cultural treasures. Indeed, the nobles appeared to have taken over the heritage of Rudolph II. The sculptor Adriaen de Vries, once the leading artist at Rudolph's Court, worked for the most opulent of these magnates, the imperial generalissimo Albrecht von Waldstein. In the halls of the palaces, picture galleries sprang into life as art collections expanded, and by the end of the seventeenth century most of them could compare favorably with the Emperor's gallery at the Castle, which was being gradually restored.

The new art center installed in the occasional seat of the Emperors at Prague Castle served to inspire the high nobility, whether foreign or of native Czech origin. By means of systematic purchases the Castle Picture Gallery was built up throughout the seventeenth century into a broadly representative collection. Though loosely linked to Rudolph's conception, it conformed to contemporary Baroque style, both in composition and in the way it was organized. Until its destruction in the middle of the eighteenth century, the effect of the Castle collection as stimulus was enhanced by the fact that it was representative of the period's society as a whole and not restricted to the person of the Emperor. Access was not limited to his Court but was open to great numbers of visitors from the Prague nobility for whose expanding efforts at collecting it must have served as a model of no small significance.

A prominent place among the seventeenth-century galleries was occupied by the Czernín Picture Gallery, founded by Humprecht Jan, Count Czernín, the "Baroque Cavalier," toward the close of the century. As the Emperor's envoy in Venice, related by marriage to the Margraves of Mantua, he was above all in touch with contemporary Mannerist Venetian art. While he made some of his art purchases through agents, he also associated personally with Venetian artists and often placed orders for specific works, generally accompanying them with instructions as to theme, composition, and treatment. His patronage found characteristic expression in the colossal and ancient Czernín Palace at Hradčany, the Palladian monumentality of which, long out of date, was literally forced upon the Count's architect, Francesco Caratti. Inside this edifice, designed to rival the magnificence of the 11

Emperor's residence at Prague Castle, the Count's art collection, which had by that time assumed remarkable proportions and earned a well-deserved name for itself, was assigned a special wing. The contents of the gallery are known, thanks to the preservation in Prague University Library of an inventory of all the paintings, consisting of 749 replicas in folio. These *Imagines galeriae* of 1669, the work of a group of artists headed by John La Fresnoy, recorded the period of the gallery's rapid growth which reached its climax at the turn of the century. After 1720, a rapid decline set in, and finally toward the end of the eighteenth century, when the family fortune was in decline, a private auction was organized and the invaluable collection amassed in the course of three generations was dispersed. Two paintings from this collection (by John La Fresnoy and Pietro della Vecchia) were transferred to the Czernín Picture Gallery in Vienna.

A significant and highly valued collection of paintings, tapestries, and weapons was assembled by the wealthy nobleman, Felix Sekerka, Count Vršovec, at his palace in Hiberna Lane in the years 1719 to 1720. However, this collection, the details of which are known from the auction catalogue that has come down to us, was not to survive its founder, and was entirely scattered in the 1720's and 1730's. Even less is known about the collection, primarily of contemporary Czech art, assembled in the years 1695 to 1720 in his *Maltézské náměstí* (Maltese Square) house by Jan Petr Straka, Count of Nedabylice, and dispersed by a sale in 1778, half a century after his death. Yet other collections of the Prague aristocracy are all but forgotten, with hardly more than the family name of their owners preserved as evidence of their existence, as for example, the Vrtba and Kolovrat families. The only exception is the picture gallery of Count Nostitz-Rieneck, which is of slightly later origin. This world-renowned collection, founded in 1736, has been preserved in its entirety to this day, its development having been essentially completed early in the nineteenth century. The early collection, the gem of which is Rembrandt's *The Rabbi*, is now housed in the National Gallery.

By the eighteenth century, Prague had absorbed the impact of an Austrian monarch, the Counter Reformation, and foreign nobles, and finally integrated Baroque culture with its own earlier expression. The effect was an unparalleled release of popular creativity in fine arts, music, and literature. *Vide* architects Christopher and Kilian Ignatius Dientzenhofer, Giovanni Aichel-Santini, and F. M. Kanka; sculptors F. M. Brokoff and M. B. Braun; painters P. Brandl and V. V. Reiner.

A host of artists followed in their footsteps. Taking full advantage of Prague's striking topography— like Rome it is built on seven hills—they reshaped the face of the city, both in large and in detail. Buildings were carefully positioned, sight lines drawn, vistas opened, façades and gables designed and worked in minute detail to conform to the new style. So consistent and pervasive was this effort that what is known as Baroque Prague almost totally concealed the old medieval core.

The eagerness of newly rich burghers to match the nobility in splendor was the chief motivating force behind Baroque Prague's transformation. The taste for the Baroque was also reflected in the burghers' private libraries and art collections. Unfortunately, the burghers' collections were short-lived, and are known through historical reference only. For example, a collection of paintings that included works by Karel Škréta and Petr Brandl was assembled in 1725 by Kašpar Friedrich, a master minter, in *Tomášskáulice* (St. Thomas Street). Jan Weidenheimb (died 1752), engrosser in the Archbishop's Consistory, put together a notable collection of 180 paintings in his fifteen-room apartment on *Maltézské náměstí* (Maltese Square). Of the other collectors whose names are recorded in the archives let us mention at least Františka Schnecková in *Pětikostelní ulice* (Street of Five Churches) and Josef, Knight of Brettfeld, professor at the Faculty of Law and Rector of Charles University in the second half of the eighteenth century. This Josef enriched his outstanding and widely acclaimed collection by judicious purchases at auctions of property belonging to monasteries that were abolished during the reign of Joseph II (1765–1790).

At the close of the eighteenth century there arose a new type of collector who tended to be guided more by historical, archeological, and educational interests than by aesthetic considerations. A prominent representative of the new breed was Karel Josef, Knight Biener of Bienenberk,

Sheriff in Hradec Králové whose official seat was in Prague. He, too, knew how to derive profit and advantage from the public auctions that resulted from Emperor Joseph's reforms, and he assembled a large collection of art objects and archeological artifacts, which, after his death in 1792, passed into the hands of the wealthy Prague printer, Jan Ferdinand Schönfeld. Inclusion of archeological findings in this collection and its exhibition in public, under the name of Schönfeld's Museum, first in Prague and from 1799 in Vienna, are evidence of a new epoch in collecting and another step forward in the development of the modern museum.

Another example of an early private collection that emphasized the instructional—including the developing interest in natural sciences—is a small collection of natural objects, weapons, artifacts, and articles of historic interest that was bought by the Premonstratensian Monastery at Strahov from Baron Karl Eben in 1798. Preserved in its original form, it is now exhibited at the Memorial of National Literature, which is housed in the former monastery.

The new kinds of collections were an outgrowth of emerging ideas concerning the power of human understanding. Known as the Enlightenment, these ideas, which emphasized objective, scientific knowledge, reached the Czech lands in the third quarter of the eighteenth century. Centers of the new thinking included the Philosophical Faculty and the Faculty of Law of Charles University, the major salons of the aristocracy (for example, the Nostitz Salon in the 1770's and 1780's and the salons of Count Kinský and Count Šternberk at the turn of the century), and the first scientific institutions where liberal aristocrats were joined by a number of enlightened priests and educated bourgeois. The first scientific journal in Bohemia, *Prager Gelehrte Nachrichten* (1771–1772) paved the way for the founding in 1775 of the Private Learned Society *(Soukromá učená společnost)*, which Emperor Joseph II elevated in 1784 to the public *Societas scientiarum bohemica*, and finally, in 1790, to the Royal Bohemian Society of Sciences *(Královská česká společnost nauk)*, which enjoyed more than 150 years of activity and was one of the precursors of the present-day Czechoslovak Academy of Sciences.

It was in the nature of sober rationalism at the close of the eighteenth century to concentrate on the natural sciences and to devote to them the first museum collections open to the public. Located in the ancient Clementinum, the two oldest museums, the *Museum mathematicum* and the *Museum naturae Pragense*, primarily served the needs of the University itself, but the public was admitted on certain days of the week. The *Museum mathematicum* was attached to the renowned Astronomical Observatory of the Clementinum, and housed a collection of clocks, planetaria, and other astronomical instruments of great historical and artistic value; the younger *Museum naturae Pragense* was essentially for mineralogy and paleontology. The latter museum was started from the large private collection of František Josef, Count Kinský, who presented it to the Charles University in 1775. Another substantial contribution was made by Ignác, Knight Born, Kinský's collaborator, who was the founder of the Private Learned Society and largely responsible for the emphasis on natural sciences in the early stages of its development. However, the influence of historians and pre-Romantics soon led to an interest in history and art as well.

The fine arts situation in Austria at the close of the eighteenth century was extremely unfavorable. Joseph II's austere rationalism supported scientific thinking and had little understanding of art, either past or present. One of the reasons, among others, was art's historic link with religion and religious institutions against which rationalism, in the name of progress and common sense, waged a bitter life-and-death struggle. The dissolution of churches and monasteries was accompanied by frequent art auctions and sales at ridiculously low prices and by outright destruction of art works. The losses suffered by libraries and art collections were a black mark on Joseph's otherwise progressive reforms.

Political factors made the situation in Bohemia—and particularly Prague—even worse than elsewhere in the Empire, as centralists in Vienna increasingly opposed any reminders of the historical independence of the Czech state. Prague Castle itself, once the seat of sovereigns, declined to the point where it was used merely to house official bodies and barely escaped the degradation of being turned into artillery barracks. Similarly the Castle Picture Gallery was neglected, and many works of art were transferred from Prague to Vienna. Finally, almost everything that was left of the formerly extensive Prague Castle collections was sold at auction for a pittance to various private collectors.

It was in this atmosphere, then, that art museums open to the public and free of the imperial imprimatur began to develop in Prague. Czech indignation and political opposition to the absolutism of the Emperor's Court reinforced widespread concern for the fate of historical art objects.

The year 1796 saw the founding of the private Society of Patriotic Friends of the Arts *(Společnost vlasteneckých prátel umeni)* in which František, Count Šternberk-Manderscheid, was instrumental. This liberal noble, a lover of the fine arts, having spent his younger days at the Manderscheid family estates in the Rhine Valley, grew up under the influence of his tutor, Canon Ferdinand F. Wallraf of Cologne, a world-famous collector of works of art. Following his example, Šternberk-Manderscheid focused his interest on both fine and applied arts (among which he included coins and medals) and soon became not only a collector but an ardent lover and promoter of art. Thus it was quite natural that he should head the group of noblemen whose aim in founding the Society of Patriotic Friends of the Arts was to withstand the actions of Joseph's Court.

The avowed purpose of the society was "the renewed promotion of art and taste." The society united prominent Czech noblemen and art lovers from the bourgeoisie. It founded a gallery and, in 1800, the Academy of Fine Arts for the education and training of young artists. The Picture Gallery's purpose was "to prevent the further destruction and exportation of paintings and other works of art."

Because of the losses suffered in the preceding years, the society could save only a meager portion of the country's art collections. Nevertheless, something like five hundred works, lent by members of the society, were assembled for the first exhibition. Thereafter the number of works exhibited in the Picture Gallery varied from year to year. Actually, for many years the Picture Gallery did not own any of the items it exhibited because its charter stipulated loan exhibitions only. Systematic growth dates from 1835 when permanent acquisitions were permitted and the number of purchases began to rise. The Picture Gallery, predecessor of the present-day National Gallery, was first located in Czernín Palace in the space vacated by the sale of the Czernín collection. Later it was moved from one nobleman's palace to another until 1814 when Šternberk Palace (the present headquarters of the National Gallery) was bought for the collection. In 1885, suitable accommodations were provided in the newly constructed Rudolphinum where the Picture Gallery's modern development began. In the 1920's the gallery's wanderings began again, and did not end until some time after the close of World War II.

The era of the Enlightenment also saw the beginnings of the National Museum in Prague. Founded in 1818, it is one of the original large, regional museums that the Austrian monarchy established in the first two decades of the nineteenth century and that used the great museums of western Europe as models. The sober interest of the Enlightenment in science and nature became enriched by the emotional ardor of the Romantics, who glorified the symbols of the nation's past. Czech patriots eagerly collected historic objects to supplement the Bohemian aristocracy's original donations. The founding of the National Museum in 1818 was a genuine landmark in the development of Czechoslovak museums. The diverse interests of its supporters dictated the multiform character of its program, and, by virtue of its position at the heart of the Czech national movement throughout the first half of the nineteenth century, it has earned a special place in the history of Czech culture.

In the nineteenth century the many departments of the National Museum comprised a single, unified institution. After a time, advancing specialization in the sciences necessitated additional diversification and the creation of new specialized departments. An ultimate change in the basic structure transformed the National Museum into an organism of autonomous units. One outcome of the National Museum's origin and evolution is the unusual manner in which its art acquisitions have been displayed. Assembled on the basis of national historic interest rather than principles of art history, art works in the nineteenth century were scattered first among the Prehistory, Classical Archeology, and Numismatic Departments and subsequently the Departments of Ethnography, Theater, and Music. From the very outset, illuminated manuscripts were deposited in the National Museum Library, which gradually accumulated a collection of extraordinary significance. The very pillars of Czech book illustration of the Gothic period are among its oldest acquisitions, with the manuscripts of the *Liber viaticus*, presented to the National Museum Library by the Archbishop of Prague in 1824, heading the list. (It should be noted that in addition to the National Museum Library, major collections of illuminated manuscripts were also assembled by the University Library, the library of St. Vitus' Chapter, and, on a smaller scale, the library of the Strahov Premonstratensian Monastery.)

In the second half of the nineteenth century, Czech interest focused on attempts in western Europe to utilize the techniques of museum collection and exhibition to encourage industrial enterprise, promote new production techniques, and improve production design and appearance.

In 1862 the Prague patron of arts and ardent promoter of economic progress, Vojta Náprstek, impressed by his visit to the Kensington Museum in London, founded a private Industrial Museum; in 1886 he used his family fortune to erect a building to house its exhibits. However, the original purpose of the museum, to represent the development of industry and trade, was relegated to the background, even while Náprstek was still alive, as the result of numerous gifts of anthropological material by Czech travelers. In time, this material predominated to such an extent that the Náprstek Museum decided to specialize in it and turned over its non-anthropological collections to other Prague museums. To honor the memory of its founder, this institution now bears the name Náprstek Museum of Asian, African, and American Cultures *(Náprstkovo muzeum asijských, afrických a amerických kultur)*. Taken over by the state in 1949, it is now an autonomous branch of the National Museum.

Despite his failure to apply them consistently himself, Náprstek's ideas on the stimulating and educational impact museum collections of applied arts could have on standards of production were taken over by some of his colleagues at the Chamber of Trade and Commerce, and, in 1885, they managed to realize them in full by founding the Museum of Decorative Art *(Uměleckoprůmyslové muzeum)*. From the outset, under the management of Karel Chytil, and particularly in the new building erected in the years 1897 to 1900, this museum made stimulating advances in the fields of exhibition and education. It soon became a leader among the large industrial arts museums established in the Czech lands in the third quarter of the nineteenth century. Through gifts of great value (above all from Vojtěch Lanna, Gustav Pazaurek, Leon Bondy) and through systematic purchases, its collections grew to such an extent that in the nearly one hundred years of its development the museum became one of the wealthiest institutions of its kind, possessing comprehensive and valuable collections in all the basic branches of both historic and modern applied arts. From the very first, pride of place has been occupied by a collection of rare glass, especially Bohemian and Venetian glass.

At the turn of the century, two further movements of the day inspired the founding of new museums. The wave of enthusiasm for municipal museums furnished the stimulus for the founding in 1883 of the Museum of the City of Prague *(Muzeum hlavního města Prahy)*. After initial confusion as to its purpose, it concentrated on documenting the historical development of the city. Archeological research made a considerable contribution to its rich collections, which include many objects of both historic and artistic value, for example, the ancient *vedute* of the city, guild products, and Gothic and Baroque sculptures.

A strong influence on the Czech museum movement in the 1890's was exerted by three national exhibitions in Prague: the Jubilee Exhibition (1891), the Ethnographic Exhibition (1895), and the Exhibition of Architecture and Civil Engineering (1898), each of which had been put together by means of an enthusiastic public campaign to collect exhibits throughout the country. The very existence of the collections and the way they had been assembled awakened increased interest and, after the exhibitions were over, encouraged the establishment of additional museums. In fact, the wide network of museums that sprang up in various districts and regions, especially in Bohemia and Moravia, has remained a characteristic feature of Czech museum development. (By the end of 1976 there were 579 museums and memorial sites in the Czechoslovak Socialist Republic, including 381 in the Czech Socialist Republic.) In Prague the first two exhibitions laid the foundations for ethnographic collections that became the core of the present Department of Ethnography of the National Museum. Similarly, the stone exhibits collected for the 15 third of these great exhibitions formed the basis of the National Museum's Lapidarium collection of Czech architectonic sculpture from the eleventh to the nineteenth century.

The tendency toward specialized museums continued in the early twentieth century. Several new museums, which were to become important components of the Czechoslovak museum network in years to come, included: the Jewish Museum (1906), the Czech Technical Museum (1908, now the National Technical Museum), and the Czech Agricultural Museum (1918). The Jewish Museum was of great significance, enriching Prague's art collections with objects of a distinctive character that frequently also had great artistic value. Important decisions had been taken on the Association's basis through the enthusiastic efforts of the early volunteers already shortly after the foundation of the museum. Yet modern development and expansion did not occur until the last three decades, when historical and social conditions were quite different.

One venture, the founding of the Modern Gallery in 1902, moved Czechoslovakia closer to the mainstream of modern art museum operation. An atmosphere of artistic ferment and the search for new forms of expressing contemporary creativity generated an urgent need to do for modern art what the Picture Gallery of the Society of Patriotic Friends of the Arts had accomplished for art of the past. The foundation for the Modern Gallery's collection was laid in the years 1900–1920, with the rise of an independent Czechoslovak Republic in 1918 somewhat accelerating the program of acquisitions. The Modern Gallery's program was shaped largely by Vojtěch Volavka, with Czech art of the nineteenth century constituting the core of the collection, rounded out by the work of contemporary Czech and European artists. Of special note was a collection of French art of the nineteenth and twentieth centuries, purchased by the state in 1923 for the Modern Gallery.

Czech independence also changed the status of the Picture Gallery of the Society of Patriotic Friends of the Arts, the wealth of whose exhibits had reached unforeseen dimensions. Most notable was the extremely valuable collection of Czech Gothic art. The society's Picture Gallery became the State Collection of Ancient Art when the state assumed ownership in 1937. Under the direction of Vincenc Kramář, a sensitive expert in historic art and an ardent lover and promoter of contemporary art, the State Collection was to grow in importance. Representative both in scope and quality, it was predestined to form, with the Modern Gallery, the core of the future National Gallery.

Liberation from Nazi Germany in 1945 marked the beginning of rapid and well-rounded development in the Czechoslovak museum movement. After the socialist state came to power in 1948, several of the first measures taken in the field of culture were devoted to museums. By a special Act of Parliament the National Gallery was established as the central repository of painting, other graphic arts, and sculpture. Gradually it was provided with the necessary housing in a number of buildings, the first among these being its former home, the Šternberk palace at Hradčany Castle, and recently in the rebuilt Georgian Convent. In quick succession the state took over other important museums in Prague: the National Museum (1949), the Museum of Decorative Art (1949), the Jewish Museum (1950), the National Technical Museum (1951), and two museums of music, the Bedřich Smetana Museum (1952) and the Antonín Dvořák Museum (1954). Further specialized museums were founded in the fifties: the V. I. Lenin Museum (1951), the Alois Jirásek Museum of Literature (1951), the Klement Gottwald Museum (1952), and the Memorial of National Literature (1953).

Finally, the legal status of all museums and galleries in the socialist society was defined in the Museums and Galleries Act of 1959. As suggested by the law's title, the term "gallery" has a special meaning in Czechoslovakia, and was applied to art museums as specialized institutions intended for the display of works of art of past and present and for the advancement of aesthetic education. At the same time, however, the passing of a single statute symbolizes the fact that, despite their distinctive features, galleries in Czechoslovakia, as elsewhere in the world, form part of a great family of museum-type institutions that are closely linked by related features in their work, whether in science, documentation, or education. The 1959 Act, in recognition of the long and distinguished history of the National Gallery and the National Museum, assigns them (and the National Technical Museum) a special role in the network of Czechoslovak museums, stipulating that each in its respective field is to be the center of scientific and methodological activity in relation to the country's other museums (or, as far as the National Gallery is concerned, in relation to the Regional and District Galleries). Subsequent legal changes in 1964 and 1976 created, as already noted, professionally autonomous branches within the National Museum.

In addition to the national museums there are also some outstanding specialized museums under central management. Some of these, situated in Prague, are important from the point of view of art history, although the artistic value of the exhibits is only one aspect of their orientation, and not the guiding principle. Thus, as already mentioned, the Memorial of National Literature, installed in the Romanesque interior of the former Strahov Monastery, has a rare historical collection containing, among other things, medieval illuminated manuscripts. In the course of its development since 1919, the Military Museum has assembled a vast assortment of exhibits whose value in documenting the history of arms and weapons is enhanced by the high artistry and craftsmanship of many pieces.

The State Jewish Museum, particularly rich in applied arts exhibits, has some unique characteristics. The scope of its collections and its rapid and extraordinary growth are due to the fact that, in the years of the Nazi occupation, the museum was flooded with valuable objects from devastated synagogues and from the properties of liquidated Jewish religious communities in Bohemia and Moravia in such overwhelming volume that the original assets of the privately funded museum were multiplied many times over. The Jewish Museum collections represent not only a concentration of Jewish ritual and ethnographic objects —the largest in the world—not only a unique and enormously rich collection, frequently of great artistic value, but also in its total impact, a frightening testimony and a warning to posterity.

Supplementing the structural framework of Prague's museums are three outstanding exhibitions of particular significance from the perspective of art history, which were installed at Prague Castle under the auspices of the President of the Republic. In 1961, the St. Vitus treasure was transferred from the cathedral vault to the Chapel of the Holy Cross in the second courtyard; modern museum techniques were used, and the installation in the larger chambers is exemplary. Not long after, the Prague Castle Picture Gallery was opened in the same courtyard. The gallery contains a selection of works preserved from the former wealth of art objects gathered at the seat of Bohemian rulers. This exhibition, the scientific reconstruction of which is the result of the pioneering work of Professor Jaromír Neumann, as already noted, represents but a fragment of the collections of Bohemian rulers. Aside from its artistic value, it is significant because of the documented evidence it provides of some aspects of the original Castle collections, including the Collection of Old Czech Art housed since 1976 in the Georgian Convent forms part of it.

It is in contemplation of the Castle Picture Gallery that one becomes aware with particular urgency of how complex and different—as compared with other royal seats—is the history of art treasures of the city of Prague. Modern Prague museums do not contain the entire body of the royal collections and treasuries, although they had originally been assembled in Prague and were among the largest and most valuable in Europe. Just as with architectural monuments, the wealth of movable art works has been grievously depleted as a result of the many fateful events in the city's thousand-year history. Nevertheless, despite wars, devastation, and plundering, despite migrations, exports, and changes in taste, politics, and philosophy, despite auctions and sales and polite "borrowing," the collecting zeal of entire generations has managed to preserve much of the creative output of Czechoslovakia. This native heritage has been enriched as well through the systematic acquisition, by individuals and museums, of precious objects of art from abroad. Thus Prague, once the treasure house of Europe, can again be rightly included among the great centers of art in the world.

NATIONAL MUSEUM

The National Museum in Prague was founded on April 15, 1818. Its origins date back to the period following the French Revolution when royal and private collections of art, science, and culture were first being made accessible to the public. Prague's National Museum is one of the Land Museums established early in the nineteenth century in different parts of the Austrian Empire. One of these museums, the Joanneum in Graz, founded in 1811, was the prototype for the Land Museums' educational programs, diversified collections, and strong political and national emphasis, the latter a product of—and reaction to—Austrian absolutism under Francis I.

Credit for founding the National Museum in Prague goes to a group of prominent noblemen, headed by Kašpar Šternberk. Deeply influenced by the Enlightenment and supported by scholars at the Royal Bohemian Society of Sciences, the nobles donated their large collections to get the museum started. Most notable were the paleontology, mineralogy, and botany collections of Kašpar Šternberk, who also became the first president of the Society of the Patriotic Museum, which was founded in 1820 and served as trustee and operator of the National Museum for more than a hundred years.

The focus on natural science in the first collections determined the character of the institution's early development. This emphasis was enhanced no doubt by the outstanding personality of Kašpar Šternberk, botanist, mineralogist, and, above all, eminent phytopaleontologist. Being a product of his times, he also had a full appreciation of curios and artistic memorabilia. This versatility certainly encouraged his warm and close friendship with Johann Wolfgang von Goethe. For his part, the poet showed his friendship through a heartfelt interest in the new museum, its journal, and its collections, which he augmented by the gift of his own collection of west Bohemian minerals in 1821.

The National Museum did not become interested in collecting historical treasures until the 1830's and 1840's, when Romanticism came to the fore and the institution was increasingly perceived as the center of Czech nationalism. The conception of a diversified program was primarily that of František Palacký, historian and secretary of the Society of the Patriotic Museum from 1841. Until then, the eager but disorganized efforts of the museum's volunteer workers, who came from all social strata, did not produce any notable acquisitions. Historical events were covered only in the fine numismatic collections—the gift of the private collection of František Šternberk-Manderscheid substantially enriched this section—and through the specialized literature, rare prints, and medieval illuminated manuscripts in the library, which was an important section of the museum from the very inception.

František Palacký tried to balance the two components, natural science and history, and in the Treatise of 1841 he described the institution's program as an effort to become "a scientific reflection of the country." He saw the museum itself as the repository of historical, cultural, and artistic documents and objects as well as natural science exhibits. In 1843, Palacký stimulated the formation of the Society's Archeological Committee, which in later years became a major collection and research center in the fields of prehistoric and classical archeology. It was also due to his initiative and under his guidance that some years earlier two highly significant publishing ventures came to fruition, greatly expanding the museum's sphere of influence. They were, in 1827, *Časopis Národního muzea (The National Museum Journal)* and, in 1831, *Matice česká*, a publishing house. These publishing activities, which brought together creative Czech scientific and literary forces, made the National Museum the focal point of contemporary national life and offered fertile ground for modern Czech science and literature to grow in.

Implementing Palacký's program was not easy, and it took almost a hundred years before the National Museum acquired historic collections that could compare with its rich, compact, and systematic collections in the natural sciences. Moreover, throughout the nineteenth century, the historical material was lumped together under the vague name of "Antiquities." The numismatic collection did not receive a curator of its own until 1881, and the remaining material was not classified until the early nineties, when it was divided into three collections: Prehistorical Archeology, Classical Archeology, and Ethnography. In the twentieth century, owing to advancing specialization, other departments were added, conforming the museum's structure to the requirements of scientific study in various fields of history.

Establishment of the three archeological sections was facilitated by the museum's finally moving to a new building of its own, after several temporary locations in noblemen's palaces. This was a major step, putting to an end many years of worry and intensive searching for permanent and suitable premises for the expanding collections. In the years 1885 to 1891, a Neo-Renaissance building, designed by architect Josef Schulz, was erected in the heart of the city in Wenceslas Square. Its decoration was the work of the most outstanding sculptors and painters of the day—the list of their names is virtually a survey of Czech fine arts at the end of the nineteenth century.

Once settled in its own building, the National Museum was able to develop its program to meet growing demands in the new century for professionalism and expertise in the execution of its work. Nevertheless, it labored under constant difficulties in finding adequate financial support, as it was entirely dependent on the National Museum Society (formerly Society of the Patriotic Museum). In 1919, the museum staff became employees of the land of Bohemia, but the museum collections and administration were not transferred until 1934. In 1922, the Ethnographic Department of the National Museum was formed by merging the National Museum ethnographic collections with those of the Czecho-Slavonic Ethnographic Museum, a property of various associations until the government took it over. Similarly, in 1932 Bohemia took over the Náprstek Museum, which specialized in the ethnography and culture of Asian, African, and American peoples, and made it part of the National Museum. New departments were also formed by dividing existing sections as specialization increased. In 1930, the Department of Theater was separated from the National Museum Library and established as an independent unit. In 1948, the music collection in the National Museum Library was combined with the collection of musical instruments in the Department of Classical Archeology, forming the new Department of Music, which in 1976 became part of the Museum of Czech Music.

The development of the National Museum between 1945 and the present time was marked by significant legal changes in structure and status. In its historical perspective and in the nature of its objectives, Prague's National Museum, by mid-century, reflected all of Czechoslovakia and not just the historic land of Bohemia. In effect, then, the museum's takeover by the national government in 1949 gave legal sanction and expression to the museum's historic mission and the actual character of its collections. The National Museum's role and its leadership among Czechoslovak museums were subsequently spelled out in the Museums and Galleries Act of 1959.

As time went on, there were further profound changes in the structure of the institution, culminating in the Statute of May 1, 1964, which turned the hitherto unitary National Museum into an organism of five professionally autonomous components: two basic units, the Museum of Natural Science and the Historical Museum, plus the Náprstek Museum of Asian, African, and American Cultures, the National Museum Library, and the Central Office of Museology. (The office is a national center of museology and provides technical assistance to the country's museums.) A sixth autonomous unit was created with the establishment of the Museum of

Czech Music in 1976. There is no separate Art Department in the National Museum; however, a vast array of objects with great artistic value can be found in the various departments of the Historical Museum, in the Náprstek Museum, in the Museum of Czech Music, and in the National Museum Library (covered in this volume in the section on illuminated manuscripts in Prague).

The new organization made it possible for the individual components to develop professionally in harmony with the specific needs and methods of their particular branches of science. At the same time, however, by preserving the name of National Museum and the central management of vital matters common to all, due consideration was given to the remarkable and historically significant tradition that had emerged in the nation's consciousness over the 150 years of the National Museum's existence.

DEPARTMENT OF PREHISTORY AND PROTOHISTORY

The National Museum's prehistoric exhibits constitute an extremely rich collection of artifacts in daily use some thousands of years ago. They provide evidence of the way life developed from paleolithic to historical times, particularly in the territory of the Czechoslovak Socialist Republic. In addition, the department also has collections in the field of classical archeology, which, though limited in scope, are of great value.

The development of archeological sciences in Czechoslovakia is closely associated with the creation and classification of the National Museum's prehistoric collections. For a full hundred years they were the sole focus of research in this discipline. Of particular importance in the development of the department was the founding of the Archeological Association in 1843 and pudlication of the journal *Památky archeologické (Archeological Monuments)*, which has been appearing since 1854 (nowadays as an organ of the Archeological Section of the Czechoslovak Academy of Sciences), and which is the oldest archeological magazine in Czechoslovakia.

The curators of the collections in the nineteenth century were also among Czechoslovakia's first archeologists. J. L. Píč (1893–1911) is credited with the country's first systematic archeological field explorations. Careful and thorough study of their findings by Píč and his associates opened the way, for the first time, to the solution of the fundamental questions of Czech and central European protohistory. The creative early work invested in the prehistoric collections and in Bohemian archeology provided successful points of departure for the twentieth-century scholars who followed. The performance of the nineteenth- and twentieth-century trail blazers was so outstanding that even today, when the system of Czechoslovak archeological museums has been decentralized and the work divided among the several institutions, the extraordinary wealth and scientific integrity of the National Museum's collections are still widely acknowledged.

It follows from the nature of archeological excavations that their documentary significance is primarily historical and cultural; any artistic merit is secondary to the function or purpose of an artifact. This is true even where the object is symbolic, as in ritual sculpture, whether paleolithic or neolithic. The primacy of the scientific significance of archeological findings, however, in no way detracts from the artistic value of the rare monuments, sculptures, ceramics, and objects of gold, bronze, and iron assembled in the prehistory collection of the National Museum. One of the most valuable, the head of a deity dating from the period of the Celt presence in Bohemia (second century B.C.) is a unique find in the field of Celtic sculpture.

The department's collection of classical antiquities is the largest of its kind in Czechoslovakia. Its main value lies in the documentation of ancient Greek and Roman arts and crafts. The collection includes a few marble busts. The sub-Mycenaean period, Geometric Style, Corinthian circle, black and red painted Attic vessels, Hellenistic ceramics, vases from southern Italy and the Kerch Peninsula, terra cottae—all are represented in the pottery collection, which is also rich in glass objects and small sculptures and vessels of bronze. The antiquities collection also includes a number of pieces of jewelry. Among the most valuable objects are a painted dish of Nikosthenes, a glass bottle of the port of Puteoli, and a gilded silver rhyton.

The mission of the Department of Classical Archeology begins where protohistory leaves off. The department has assembled objects that trace the cultural and historical development of Czechoslovakia, with most of the exhibits in its collections from Bohemia. The collections, which are among the oldest in the National Museum, were part of the unvariegated exhibits of the museum's early days. It was not until the end of the nineteenth century that they were scientifically classified and organized.

In the course of the collections' development over 150 years, the conception, too, has undergone various changes. Palacký's program of 1841, calling for the museum to be a reflection of the country's natural conditions, history, and culture, narrowed the museum's area of interest geographically but at the same time defined the range of its objectives so broadly that it could hardly be implemented. There were other problems. The starting point for most large European museums was the collection of the Royal Court, but there was no such collection intact in Prague, as already explained in the Introduction. Furthermore, from the very outset, other collections and museums seemed to preempt one area after another of Palacký's program for the National Museum. As early as 1796, the Society of Patriotic Friends of the Arts was dealing systematically with the fine arts, putting together collections that eventually formed the basis of the National Gallery. In the twentieth century, advancing specialization led to new museums which competed with one another—and the National Museum—for exhibits. Professor J. Koula, who headed the department from 1892 to shortly after World War I, did much to enlarge the department's collections. Koula, however, favored the field of arts and crafts and was at a competitive disadvantage vis-à-vis the Museum of Decorative Art, which had been carrying out its program of acquisitions since 1885. For the last fifty years or so, however, those in charge of the Department of Classical Archeology have reverted to an historical emphasis; objects of fine art have been added to existing collections, but the decisive criterion for any new acquisition has been its historical significance.

From this perspective, various collections as well as individual exhibits testify to the development of both urban and rural culture in the Middle Ages. Of particular value are the collections of medieval ceramics. A special place in the collection of medieval objects is occupied by weapons and shields linked with the Hussite movement of the fifteenth century. They provide considerable historical documentation on this important period in Bohemian history. Also of great value are collections of historical and cultural items dating from the Renaissance and Baroque periods and objects recalling outstanding figures of Czech culture in the period of National Revival.

Apart from their historical significance, many of these objects possess a considerable, sometimes a very high, artistic value. Examples worthy of particular attention are: a silver tiara from the twelfth century adorned with reliefs and pendants; medieval, Renaissance, and Baroque jewels; medieval liturgical objects (especially the reliquary of St. Eligius in the shape of a mitre, an excellent work of Prague goldsmiths from the days of Charles IV); Gothic and Renaissance glazed tiles and paving stones; the precious embroidered Rosenberg antependium dating from the second half of the fourteenth century; Gothic stained glass paintings, reliefs, and sculptures; fifteenth-century painted medieval shields (*paveses*); guild products of the fifteenth to eighteenth century; and fine Bohemian pewter, glass, and porcelain from the eighteenth and nineteenth centuries.

Items of extraordinary artistic value, assembled in the Lapidarium of the National Museum, include a collection of Bohemian architectonic sculptures, ranging from the eleventh to the nineteenth century. The latter collection, one of the bases of the Department of Classical Archeology, dates from the very beginning of the National Museum and the crystallization of its historical role in the first half of the nineteenth century.

The first stone sculptures and architectonics were obtained as early as the 1840's, but it was the retrospective national exhibitions of the 1890's, mentioned in the Introduction, that made decisive contributions to the growth and integration of the Lapidarium collections. Of particular importance was the third, the Exhibition of Architecture and   22

Civil Engineering of 1898, which documented the development of historical styles in an impressive display of a great number of items, both originals and copies. The collection was preserved after the exhibition ended, and the pavilion where it had been installed became its permanent home, becoming the Lapidarium of the National Museum. The collection was enlarged and freshly installed in 1905, and again, after merging with the stone exhibits of the City Museum, in 1910. New installations of the ever-growing collection were carried out in 1932 and, finally, in 1954.

The objects in the Lapidarium are exhibited in chronological order according to stylistic development. Of particular worth is the Romanesque group, which has been enriched in quantity, quality, and variety by Czech archeological excavations in such locations as Prague Castle. Also notable is a number of sculptured figurines of the Romanesque period. The Oldřiš relief from the mid-twelfth century is the first attempt in Bohemia to preserve a set of figures of close to monumental size. The late Romanesque statue of lions in Kouřim is the first Bohemian free-standing sculpture; it dates from the early thirteenth century and is a fine work of art, harmoniously combining the natural shape with the stylistic discipline of Romanesque style.

The Lapidarium has examples from Prague and Kolín of the early period of Gothic architectonic sculptures. The Parléř group of the second half of the fourteenth century is represented by decorative sculptures from St. Vitus' Cathedral and fragments from the northern portal of Týn Church. Another interesting group consists of tombstones from the former monastery at Ostrov. Fragments from the Old Town Hall in Prague and from St. Barbara's Cathedral in Kutná Hora are relics of Late Gothic architecture and sculpture. Finally, there is the figure of a knight, erected in the early sixteenth century on a pillar of Charles Bridge to symbolize the rights of the Lesser Quarter (it was also referred to as the Prague Roland, or Bruncvík).

Of Renaissance architecture, a group of decorative fragments and several portals from burgher houses in Prague have been preserved in the Lapidarium. Stylistic developments in sculpture of the period are represented by close to thirty decoratively ornamented tombstones, by house reliefs, and by remnants of the fine red marble fountain that used to embellish the main square of the Old Town of Prague. This outstanding work, which dates from 1591, is ornamented with decorative sculpture and figurines in the familiar Italian Mannerist style.

Of particular richness and value is the Lapidarium's group of Baroque stone sculptures in which Prague's most significant works of the period are represented. The chain starts with St. Mary's Column from the Old Town Square (1650) by Jan Jiří Bendl and culminates in the works of sculptors who contributed to the world-famous decoration of Charles Bridge: Jan Brokoff *(Baptism of Christ,* 1706), Ottavio Mosto *(St. Wenceslas,* 1700), F.M. Brokoff *(St. Ignatius of Loyola* and *St. Francis Xaverius,* 1711), and Matyáš B. Braun *(St. Ivo,* 1711). In addition to these original statues from Charles Bridge, the Lapidarium contains other pieces from the workshops of these Baroque masters of Prague, including the *Virgin Mary* (1726) from the column on Hradčany Square by F.M. Brokoff and a number of works from the atelier of Matyáš B. Braun— *Atlas* (about 1720) from the Vrtba Garden *(Vrtbovská zahrada)* in the Lesser Quarter, the statue of *Emperor Charles VI* (1720 to 1725), and six garden sculptures from the J. V. Michna summer house in the New Town of Prague (1712 to 1720). Bohemian Rococo is represented in the Lapidarium by J. M. Brüderle's fountain (1739) from the Loreto courtyard in Prague, while the classicism of the 1760's is represented by two allegorical figures, the work of Ignác F. Platzer, from the attic of the Kinský Palace in the Old Town Square. In addition to these outstanding works of Bohemian Baroque, the Lapidarium has many examples of sculptured decorations from Prague façades and gables, garden sculptures and vases, architectonic objects, portals, tombstones, and the like.

The exposition is rounded out by items from the nineteenth century, among which the most valuable are the statue of *Venus* from the fountain in the palace of Bishop Thun in Prague and two busts by the Prague sculptor, Josef Malínský, which are interesting for their realistic rendering of simple, popular figures.

The contribution of Vojta Náprstek, patron of the arts and innovator in production methods, design, and display, was traced in the Introduction. Náprstek was a strong believer in the value of museums, and in his lifetime had the satisfaction of playing a major role in two of Prague's leading museums. In 1885, the Museum of Decorative Art was launched with the help of industrial arts exhibits contributed by the private museum Náprstek had established nearly twenty-five years earlier in 1862. At the same time, his private museum committed itself to its growing ethnographic and cultural collections, becoming the Náprstek Museum of Asian, African, and American Cultures. It became part of the National Museum in 1932, and is now one of the National Museum's autonomous units.

Since the 1930's the museum has concentrated more and more on non-European ethnography. The foundations for this area of specialization were laid by material assembled by Czech explorers, some of whose trips were underwritten by Vojta Náprstek. Some additions were made during the period between the two world wars. Since 1945, the collections have grown so rapidly in number and value that today they cover, though not in balanced proportions, ethnographically and culturally important regions on all non-European continents. Almost all these additions have one shortcoming in common: They did not derive from the museum's own research activities but were acquired as gifts, purchases, or transfers from other properties. An institution's own carefully monitored research is the only way to provide accurate data essential for classifying and scientifically ordering its holdings. This deficiency has been gradually overcome in recent years, thanks to the new conception of the institution's role and the expert work of qualified specialists in the individual branches of the museum's program.

The museum's present program is not focused on ethnography alone. Side by side with many factual exhibits on their way of life are priceless specimens of artistic creations by non-European peoples. In these cultures, both components—daily living and artistry—are indissolubly linked and tend to complement each other. It is hardly possible to explain fully the essence of the artistic creativity without regard for its connection with specific individual features of the people's lives. In the same way, any conceptualization of their way of life would be incomplete without the artistic component. Prompted by this conviction and the desire to characterize the collections accurately, the new curators changed the name of "Náprstek Museum of Ethnography" to "Náprstek Museum of Asian, African, and American Cultures." In this field, the museum has developed successful cooperation with kindred institutions abroad.

From the perspective of the development of Oriental art, the collection of the writer Joe Hloucha, is the most important in the Náprstek Museum. The museum acquired it gradually by purchases in 1936 and 1943 and by a bequest Hloucha arranged shortly before his death in 1957. Most numerous in the collection are specimens of Far Eastern art, but the most important items scientifically and the most valuable artistically are in the African collection, of which African dance masks form the most interesting and valued part. This collection of African art is the best of the Náprstek Museum's extensive and fine art exhibits. Its quality is evidenced by the fact that seven of its exhibits were selected to be shown at the International Exhibition of Traditional African Art, held on the occasion of the First World Festival of African Art in Dakar in 1966. It was at this exhibition, later transferred to Paris, that the unique pair of human figures from the Northeast Congo was displayed.

Apart from Hloucha's collection, other items were gradually acquired by the museum from the collections of A. Sachs (1926), J. Golovin (1935), J. Maternová (1946), and F. V. Foit (1947).

With regard to American cultures, the Náprstek Museum possesses a small but significant collection of tribal art from the Northwest Coast of North America. It originated in the collection assembled by Phillip Oberländer in the first decade of the twentieth century. In the Oceania group, Durdík's collection from the Nias Island, dating from the 1880's, is the most significant.

DEPARTMENT OF ETHNOGRAPHY

The Department of Ethnography aims to gather systematically factual material about the history and culture of the people of Czechoslovakia and of other, chiefly Slavonic, nations of Europe from the end of the seventeenth century to the present day, with the emphasis, of course, on Czechoslovakia. Since the beginning of the twentieth century, the non-Czechoslovak Slavonic collections have focused primarily on Balkan culture, so that today the department can boast of extensive and systematic collections from Bulgaria and Yugoslavia (particularly Serbia). The remaining Slavonic groups are less comprehensive and systematically assembled, although a collection of items on the people of the southwest Ukraine, especially the Hutsuls, is especially fine.

The historical basis of the collection was provided by two great national exhibitions organized toward the end of the nineteenth century. The oldest ethnographic collections of the National Museum are a heritage of the Jubilee Exhibition of 1891. At first the Jubilee exhibits were incorporated in the Department of Classical Archeology, but after the great Ethnographic Exhibition in Prague in 1895, many of the items assembled for the exhibition, including some of the Jubilee exhibits, were taken over by the Czecho-Slavonic Ethnographical Museum (Spolkové národopisné muzeum československé), which was established at the time. The collections were first housed in the Sylva-Taroucca Palace in Na Příkopě Street. In 1902, Count Kinský's former summer residence was acquired for them. In 1922, however, the museum was taken over by the government of Bohemia and merged with the ethnographic collections of the National Museum in a separate Department of Ethnography, which has carried on its work in the Kinský summer house right up to the present day. Another reshuffling occurred in 1943 when the Náprstek Museum's extensive collections in Slavonic ethnography, the Museum of Decorative Art's collection of folk art, and various other exhibits were transferred to the National Museum's Department of Ethnography. The department's current collecting and research activities are adding valuable material relating to forms of rural life that have been disappearing in the last few decades.

In concept, the permanent exhibition of the Department of Ethnography, as remounted in 1964, is intended to demonstrate, through typical examples, changes in the main areas of people's lives and to trace the development of folk culture. In folk culture, artistic expression is not limited to art qua art but is evident in practical objects of everyday life.

Despite the fact that the decisive criterion in selecting the exhibits for the 1964 reinstallation was their ethnographic worth and not their artistic value, varied and remarkable examples of folk art abound. The individuality of folk art in Czechoslovakia and the diversity of its creative inventiveness can be seen in all the ethnographic collections—folk costumes and embroideries, wooden furniture, ceramics, folk sculptures, and stained glass. The Czech and Slovak costumes and embroideries are among the richest and most beautiful in central Europe. One can even find samples of unique seventeenth-century folk embroideries in which ancient heraldic designs are executed in multicolored silks. Later items, originating in Moravia and Slovakia, are characterized by outstanding designs and colors, while Czech needlework often covers a garment or cloth with open work in such a way that it looks like precious lace. More than twenty of the most popular costumes covering the major periods of development in the various regions of Czechoslovakia bear witness to the variety of folk costumes and the people's sense of harmonious composition in the individual articles and colors.

Simple objects made of wood—furniture in a farm household, tools, or objects made by shepherds—are impressive in their simple, functional design and occasional sober carved ornaments. Great artistic value is found in the painted and inlaid folk furniture and in the limitlessly varied figure motifs of gingerbread molds.

Variety in shape and ornament is equally characteristic of folk ceramics, whether the simpler earthenware from Bohemia or the painted faïence products from Moravia and western Slovakia, which are a creative continuation of Renaissance faïence, adopted as folk art in these regions during the late seventeenth and early eighteenth centuries. Rich fantasy also lent individual and impressive form to many items of folk custom, for example, 25

Shrovetide carnival masks, painted Easter eggs, and pictures and sculptures of the Nativity. It was expressed, too, in pure creations of folk art, such as stained glass and folk sculptures of the saints. Stained glass was especially important in a few centers near glassmakers' furnaces, and represents one of the most attractive and most eagerly sought products of the people's creative powers.

DEPARTMENT OF NUMISMATICS

The Department of Numismatics aims to achieve a complete collection of coins that have been legal tender in the past in the territory of the present-day Czechoslovak Socialist Republic. In addition, the department exhibits extensive collections of foreign coins, the most valuable being a collection of coins of classical antiquity. In their 150 years of development, the various collections have grown into a very valuable and extensive assemblage that is unique in Czechoslovakia. Besides coins, the museum also has a large and extremely valuable collection of medals.

The numismatic collections are among the earliest acquisitions of the National Museum. In 1830, a particularly significant addition to the early exhibits came with the gift of Count František Šternberk-Manderscheid's large private collection containing about four thousand items of the most valuable minted coins from Bohemia, Moravia, and Silesia, including 261 gold coins and 3,079 silver coins. This enthusiastic patron of the arts and founder of the Society of Patriotic Friends of the Arts devoted to the assembling of his collection fifty years of ardent collecting, genuine expert knowledge, and a great deal of money. His private collection came to include other significant collections of his day, particularly the celebrated collection that had once been the property of Count E. A. Valdštejn, Bishop of Litoměřice. This collection had served as the basis for the key work in Bohemian numismatics by Voigt, entitled *Beschreibung der böhmischen Münzen (Description of Bohemian Coins)*.

The Šternberk gift thus was the foundation for the subsequent growth of the museum's numismatic collections.

In the course of the nineteenth century, numerous donations by many different individuals and groups enriched the numismatic collections to such an extent that in 1881, the year Professor Josef Smolík was appointed curator, the work became increasingly specialized and a separate museum department was created. Under Smolík's successors, the department evolved as Czechoslovakia's center of numismatics, noted for its systems of classification and scientific treatment of the exhibits. The growth of the department's collections, which was particularly rapid after 1945, has contributed to the world-wide reputation of the Department of Numismatics.

Today the National Museum's numismatic collection contains about half a million items. It has great value in the study of money as a means of exchange and as a significant factor in economic history. The exhibits of Bohemian coins, particularly of dinars from the Romanesque period of the Přemyslide dynasty and thaler minting dating from the sixteenth to eighteenth century, are also of interest to art historians.

Art values are also found in the department's systematically assembled collection of medals. The exhibits represent a continuous survey of the history of striking medals in Bohemia and the world over. The most valuable are Renaissance medals created by such prominent artists as Antonio Abondio and Severin Brachmann.

MUSEUM OF CZECH MUSIC

The Museum of Czech Music was established in 1976 through the merger of the Bedřich Smetana Museum, the Antonín Dvořák Museum, and the National Museum's Department of Music. It is the sixth autonomous unit of the National Museum.

The National Museum's Department of Music was part of the National Museum Library as far back as 1819, the year after the museum's founding. In the course of the nineteenth century, the library gathered together manuscripts and printed copies of both vocal and instrumental compositions, with special attention devoted to works by leading Czech composers. In 1948, this collection was detached from the library and became the basis for a new department whose program was extended by collections of librettos, correspondence, and musical instruments. Under Alexander Buchner, who first organized the department, the collections grew to such an extent that it was necessary to acquire new premises for them outside the main museum building in what used to be the Grand Priory Palace in the Lesser Quarter, where extensive archives and a large collection of musical instruments are assembled. Summer concerts of old music are regularly performed in a garden adjoining the palace.

The collection of musical instruments dates from 1949 when a group of instruments was taken over from the Department of Classical Archeology of the National Museum. Within a few years it grew to such proportions that today it comprises about 2,300 exhibits. Of value primarily for the study of music history, the collection has many pieces of fine artistic design and workmanship. Keyboard and string instruments are interesting because of their shape and the carved surface of some parts or, in the more sophisticated pieces, the ornamented inlaid surface. The design, construction, and ornamentation of a special group of automatic devices (musical cabinets, clocks, boxes, and the like) illustrate cultural trends of the eighteenth and nineteenth centuries.

DEPARTMENT OF THEATER

The Department of Theater, originally part of the National Museum Library, was set up as a separate section in 1930. Its first collections were based primarily on the archives of two prominent Prague theaters, the National Theater and the Theater Vinohrady. In the program of acquisitions undertaken by the department's founder, Jan Bartoš, a dramatist, and his successor Josef Knap, an author, the collections were greatly expanded. Today the Department of Theater contains extensive exhibits on the history of the theater, stage and costume designs by prominent Czech artists, photographs, theater notices and posters, public records, music, memorabilia, and items from the Czech puppet theater. The department's library has both dramatic works and specialized literature about the theater. The continuing growth of the department's collections is a reflection of the importance attached to the theater throughout Czech history.

The stagecraft collections contain stage and costume designs primarily from the middle of the nineteenth century to the present day, but enriched by some exhibits from the eighteenth century. Systematic efforts are being made to round out the collections with examples of historical and contemporary creativity in equal measure. The result is a valuable gallery of Czech fine art which has influenced the contemporary theater by offering a forum for cooperation by everyone working in the theater—playwrights, actors, producers, directors, and stage and costume designers.

The puppet collection, tracing the historical role of puppet theater from the period of the National Revival through to its present-day popularity, includes historical puppets of the wandering puppeteers who carried on the tradition of the famous Matěj Kopecký, as well as modern puppets. It was found that historical puppets were created by artists prominent in other branches of the fine arts.

DESCRIPTION OF ILLUSTRATIONS

1 *Bronze Hatchet with Disk-like Back and Pair of Cuff-like Bracelets.* Hatchet: Site of find unknown. Bracelets: Libčeves near Bílina. Barrow culture of Middle Bronze Age. Second half of 2nd millennium B.C. Length of hatchet 25.5 cm. No Inv. No. Width of bracelets 4.5 and 3 cm. Inv. Nos. 10 751 and 10 752

2 *Argillite Sculpture of Head of Celtic Deity.* Mšecké Žehrovice near Nové Strašecí. Beginning of Late La Tène Age. End of 2nd century B.C. Height 22.1 cm

3 *Gold Chain with Medallion and Small Silver Plate with Relief of Stag, from Slavonic Barrow.* Želénky near Duchcov. 9th century A.D. Medallion: Height 3.9 cm, width 2.7 cm. Plate: Height 4.9 cm, width 6.7 cm. Inv. Nos. 118 743, 118 744

4 *Bronze Cup.* Lžovice near Kolín. Urn field culture of Late Bronze Age. First half of 1st millennium B.C. Height including handle 15.1 cm. Old Collection: Inv. No. 7436

5 *Bronze Mask-like Brooch with Inlay on Bow.* Chýnov near Prague. Early La Tène Age. 4th century B.C. Length 7.1 cm. Old Collection: Inv. No. 6127

6 *Bronze Figure of Boar.* Prague, Šárka. Late La Tène Age. 1st century B.C. Length 11.5 cm. Old Collection: Inv. No. 3052

7 *Earthenware Sculpture of Bull.* Slaný, Slánská hora (Slaný Mountain). Únětice culture of Early Bronze Age. First half of 2nd millennium B.C. Length 8.9 cm. Old Collection: Inv. No. 4711

8 *Two Eight-like Scrolls of Gold Wire.* Černilov near Hradec Králové. Lusatian culture of Late Bronze Age. End of 2nd millennium B.C. Length of scrolls 9 cm and 9.7 cm. Inv. Nos. 118936, 118937

9 *Bronze Figure of Trumpeter (?).* Stradonice near Beroun. Late La Tène Age. 1st century B.C. Height 4.8 cm. Berger Collection: Inv. No. C 9h

10 *Two Bronze Hatchets of Křtěnov Type.* Barrow culture of Middle Bronze Age. Beginning of second half of 2nd millennium B.C. Křtěnov, village Březí near Týn on the Vltava, district České Budějovice. Lengths 23.6 cm and 23.5 cm. Inv. Nos. 13223, 13224

11 *Třeboň Antependium (Detail).* Bohemia. About 1380. Embroidery of multicolored silk on linen ground, in split stitch. With half figures of Christ, apostles, prophets, and others. With arms of the Rožmberk family. Height 60 cm, width 120 cm. Purchased in 1931 from Figdor Collection in Vienna. Inv. No. 60756

12 *Pavese (Hussite War Shield).* Central Bohemia (Kutná Hora). Mid-15th century. Painting in distemper on wood. Shows fight between David and Goliath and inscribed with Hussite Song. Height 88.5 cm, width 47.5 cm. Inv. No. 27

13 *Last Supper.* Bohemian Master. About 1500. From former Bethlehem Chapel in Prague. Relief. Lime wood, original gilding and polychromy. Height 159.5 cm, width 157 cm. Inv. No. 60800

14 *Guild Goblet of Goldsmiths of Prague Lesser Quarter.* Prague. 16th century. Gilded copper with engraved and hammered decoration. Cuppa made of coconut. Height 22.5 cm. Acquired 1931 from Figdor Collection in Vienna. Inv. No. 60761

15 *Romanesque Coronet.* Discovered in 1937 in old river bed of Vltava near České Budějovice, Bohemia. First half of 12th century. Thin silver plate, with figures of rulers, with pendants. Embossed work. Height 9.2 cm, length 54.7 cm Inv. No. 60770

16 *Aquaemanale in Form of Fabulous Animal.* Hradec Králové, Bohemia. 12th century. Bronze. Height 26.5 cm, length 27 cm. Inv. No. 1960

17 *Romanesque Tile with Griffin.* Prague, Vyšehrad. 12th century. Baked clay. Height 20.5 cm, width 23.2 cm. Inv. No. 107184

18 *Stove Tile with Equestrian Figure of Hussite War Leader, Jan Žižka of Trocnov.* Prague, Old Town. First half of 15th century. Baked clay. Height 19 cm, width 19 cm. Inv. No. 17524

19 a *Guild Flagon of United Guild of Bakers, Millers, and Gingerbread Makers of Town of Slaný.* Bohemia. 1577. Pewter, with engraved decorations, figures, and inscription. Height 57.5 cm. Inv. No. 68829

19 b *Detail of Engraving and Inscription*

20 *Glass Tankard.* Bohemia. 1579. Enameled glass with arms of family Koc of Dobrš and with Czech inscriptions. Height 30.2 cm, diameter 15.3 cm. Inv. No. 8527

21 *Book-shaped Bottle with Screw Cap.* R. Mayss, Horní Slavkov (Schlaggenwald). Second half of 17th century. Pewter, engraved. Height 25 cm, width 17 cm. Inv. No. 5320

22 *St. Matthew with Angel.* Matyáš Bernard Braun. First third of 18th century. Bozetto. Baked clay. Height 26 cm. Inv. No. 3798

23 *Two Figures: Standing Man and Standing Woman.* Zaïre, Azande tribe. 20th century. Wood. Heights 34.5 and 35 cm. Inv. Nos. 39254, 39255

24 *Sculpture. Tutelary Deity.* Red Indians of Northwest Coast of North America. Colored wood with feathers. Height 75 cm. Inv. No. 22594

25 *Uli Figure.* Melanesia, New Ireland. 19th century. Wood, colored. Height 132.7 cm. Inv. No. 26640

26 *Head of Buddha.* India, Gandhara. 2nd to 3rd century. Gray schist. Height 26 cm. Inv. No. 16601

27 *Horse at Stake.* China. Hanging scroll. Colored inks on silk; later copy of original ascribed to Chao Meng-fu (1254 to 1322). Two seals: 1. I Tzu-sun 2. Chao Ts'ang-shi. Height 65 cm, width 44 cm. Inv. No. 17900

28 *Figure-shaped Scraper.* Peru (South America). Inca period. Bronze. Height 9.3 cm. Inv. No. 45706

29 *Portrait of Buddhist Priest (Fragment).* Japan. 16th century (?). Wood. Height 18 cm. Inv. No. 23443

30 *Faïence Jug.* Painted green, yellow, and blue in floral and geometrical design with animal figures and owner's name JOZEF BANIC. Dated 1726. Height 28.5 cm, diameter of bottom 12.5 cm. Inv. No. 178/64

31 *Painted Cupboard.* Bohemia, Krkonoše. Early 19th century. Height 172 cm, width 105 cm. Inv. No. 30580
On left: *Detail of Painted Decoration*

32 *Christ on Cross.* South Bohemia. End of 18th century. Wood, polychromy, damaged and partly restored. Height 78 cm, width 56 cm. Inv. No. 41367

33 *Črpák—Shepherd's Wooden Milk Dipper.* Central Slovakia. Mid-19th century. Handle engraved with figure of shepherd milking sheep. Held together by copper band at bottom. Height 7.5 cm, diameter 11 cm. Inv. No. 47005

34 *Gingerbread Form.* West Moravia, neighborhood of Jihlava. Beginning of 19th century. Hard wood, carved figure of hussar on horseback. Height 31 cm, width 19 cm. Inv. No. 56566

35 *Flight to Egypt.* South Bohemia. Beginning of 19th century. Glass painting. Height 50 cm, width 39 cm. Inv. No. 3991

36 *Embroidery. Detail from Hanging for Woman in Confinement.* South Moravia. End of 18th century. Colored silk thread on raw linen. Whole hanging: Length 166 cm, width 30 cm. Inv. No. 54741

37 *Embroidery. Detail of Kerchief.* Central Bohemia, neighborhood of Prague. Beginning of 19th century. White on tulle. Whole kerchief: Length 150 cm, width 150 cm. Inv. No. 2300

38 *Hurdy-gurdy.* Bohemia. 18th century. Carved scene of *Revelation of Mary* on lid. Inv. No. 1020, 745 E

39 *Clavicembalo (Harpsichord).* Bohemia. 17th century. Richly inlaid case of Caucasian walnut, painting on inside of lid. Case covered with mother-of-pearl and tortoise shell. From Rožmberk Castle. Inv. No. 974

40 Bohemia, *Duke Břetislav I* (1034-1055), Denarius, obverse, AR, diameter 2 cm

41 Bohemia, *Duke Bořivoj II* (1100-1107, 1109-1110, 1118 to 1120), Denarius, from years 1100-1110, reverse, AR, diameter 1.5 cm

42 Bohemia, *Duke Vladislav I* (1109-1118, 1120-1125), Denarius, from years 1109-1118, reverse, AR, diameter 1.5 cm

43 a Bohemia, *Duke Vladislav I* (1109-1118, 1120-1125), Denarius, from years 1120-1125, AR, diameter 1.7 cm

43 b Reverse

44 Bohemia, *King Vladislav II* (Duke 1140-1158, King 1158-1174), Denarius, from years 1158-1174, with picture of Queen Judith, reverse, AR, diameter 1.5 cm

45 Bohemia, *King Vladislav II* (Duke 1140-1158, King 1158 to 1174), Denarius, from years 1158-1174, reverse, AR, diameter 1.5 cm

46 a *Last Supper*, undated medal of Concz Welcz (1527-1533), obverse AR, diameter 7.9 cm
b Reverse

47 a *Leonard and Barbara Harrach*, undated medal of Antonio Abondio (?-1591), AR, diameter 3.8 cm
b Reverse

48 *Prudenczy Myslíkowá*, undated medal of Severin Brachmann (?-1590), obverse, AR, diameter 3.4 cm

49 *Adam Myslík of Hýřšov*, undated medal of Severin Brachmann (?-1590), from 1573, obverse, AR, diameter 3.4 cm

50 a *King Ferdinand III*, undated medal of Alessandro Abondio (1580-1648), obverse, diameter 4.3 cm
b Reverse

51 Coronation medal of *Charles VI and Elisabeth Christina*, coined in Prague in 1723 by G. W. Vestner and A. Vestner, reverse, AR, diameter 4.4 cm

52 Josef Wenig: Costume designs for Shakespeare's *Macbeth* (National Theater, Prague, 1916, directed by Jaroslav Kvapil)

53 František Tröster: Stage model for Shakespeare's *Julius Caesar* (National Theater, Prague, 1936, directed by Jiří Frejka)

NATIONAL GALLERY

The National Gallery, the finest and most respected museum of fine art in the Czechoslovak Socialist Republic is, by Act of Parliament in 1949, responsible for collecting and safeguarding works of art, providing technical and scientific care, and making the collections accessible to the public.

Since the early nineteenth century, fine art has moved away from the private halls of the few and royal to large, publicly supported museums and galleries. In Czechoslovakia, successive generations have recognized the contributions these institutions have made to the growth of artistic creativity and the nation's cultural development. Although interest in art trailed behind music, drama, and literature in the 1800's and early 1900's, it did not take fine art long to catch up, according to the evidence provided by numerous artists, art critics, scientists, and writers of succeeding decades. Even more significant, perhaps, is Prague itself, which through the perils and frequently tragic events of history lost many of its rich art treasures but whose walls and streets, palaces, churches, and cathedrals testify to the ancient artistic traditions of the country.

The National Gallery is divided into four sections: Ancient Art, Modern Art, Graphic Art, and Oriental Art. These extensive collections were started at different times, and each has a character and history of its own. The long story of the origin and gradual development of the National Gallery reflects both the growth of Czech national culture and the struggles waged during the nineteenth and twentieth centuries to preserve and promote the fine arts. During this period, the patronage of the nobility yielded to that of the bourgeoisie, which, in turn, gave way to support from the First Republic (lukewarm for the most part) and now from the Czechoslovak socialist state, which makes a strong, conscious effort to promote and safeguard this outstanding institution.

Largest and finest of the sections, the Collection of Ancient Art constitutes the core of the National Gallery collections. In addition, it occupies pride of place in the development of modern Czech museology, embodying the tradition that started in the National Gallery's earliest days.

The collection grew originally out of a symbiosis between Enlightenment endeavors to provide culture for all and Romanticism's nostalgia for the values of the past. The initiative for its founding in 1796 was taken by the Society of Patriotic Friends of the Arts established and presided over by František, Count Šternberk-Manderscheid. This predominantly aristocratic group, which included a few burghers, was animated by the spirit of patriotism, and vowed to renew the traditional importance of Prague as capital of the Kingdom of Bohemia, to overcome the long stagnation in the country's artistic creativity, and to prevent further wholesale exports of works of art like those that had impoverished Bohemia during the seventeenth and eighteenth centuries. The newly founded Society of Patriotic Friends of the Arts undertook to realize its intentions in several ways: An art school was started in 1799–1800, shortly after the establishment of the Picture Gallery—in time the school was to become the Academy of Fine Arts—, the year 1825 saw establishment of the Fine Arts Association (*Krasoumná jednota*), whose aim was to promote contemporary creative efforts through regular exhibitions, publication of graphic prints, direct commissions to all kinds of artists, and so on.

The society's Picture Gallery grew out of rather modest beginnings. Possessing no exhibits of its own, 31 it had to rely on loans from noblemen's private collections, while occasional works bought by the society were generally made part of a lottery among its members, hence the haphazard character of the relatively extensive yet unsystematically assembled collection, which necessarily changed frequently. It was not until 1835, when the above practices were abandoned and works, whether purchased or donated, could be retained as permanent acquisitions, that the actual history of the Picture Gallery and its collections began. Naturally enough, the growth of the gallery's collections was still only gradual and fortuitous, the sources being donations from noblemen's collections and occasional acquisitions from churches and cathedrals, eked out here and there by purchases from exhibitions. For some reason, the art trade did not prosper in Bohemia, and works were seldom acquired through the trade. A particularly valuable asset was the long-term loan of a number of paintings surviving from the art collections at Prague Castle. The gallery was also substantially enriched by the gift in 1843 of a large collection assembled by Dr. Josef Hoser. The Castle and Hoser items thus acquired form the basis of the National Gallery exhibits to this very day.

A problem facing the Picture Gallery from the outset was that of finding suitable premises. In this, too, it had to depend on the good will of several noble patrons in whose palaces it found temporary shelter. From 1810, the society contemplated the erection of a building of its own for the Picture Gallery. In 1811, however, the Šternberk Palace, close to Hradčany Castle, was purchased, and the collection found a home there for the next six decades (1814–1871). In fact, it is the very same building where, by historical coincidence, the National Gallery permanently moved its Collection of Ancient Art in 1945. In the 1860's and 1870's, the idea of having a building specially erected was revived; unfortunately, however, to the detriment of the collections' future, the plan was dropped, and the design that had been worked out to meet all the gallery's requirements and that incorporated the best features of the day was never put into effect.

In 1885, a new chapter in the Picture Gallery's history began when it found a worthy home in the fine Neo-Renaissance concert hall of the Rudolphi-num built by Josef Zítek and Josef Schulz, a gift of the Bohemian Savings Bank to Prague cultural life. The new location offered the conditions necessary for the consolidation and, more important, the gradual expert classification of the collection. Up to this time it had been mixed or even confused in character, with unreliable attributions (including, as one can read in old catalogues, many a famous name taken in vain).

The curator of the Picture Gallery collection in this period was Viktor Barvitius, in his young years a promising painter and a man holding modern views (in his studies and sketches he was very close to Impressionism). Barvitius was well versed in theoretical museology and a man of wide horizons. Thanks to his efforts, in cooperation with experts from abroad—particularly Wilhelm Bode—the collection was classified with considerable insight. It was also due to Barvitius that it gradually acquired a clear character of its own and that the first catalogue based on scientific principles was published in 1889, with a comprehensive introduction on the history of the Picture Gallery. These activities continued under their own momentum during the stewardship of Pavel Bergner, Barvitius' successor, who concentrated his efforts on a thorough conservation of the collection rather than further refining its character and completing its organization on a professional basis.

At the turn of the century, then, the Picture Gallery was stable enough, but still had no adequate program for the future, lacking as it did an active and fruitful relationship with the mainstream of Czech cultural development. Feudal-dynastic, regional-patriotic interests had long outlived their time; the Society of Patriotic Friends of the Arts no less than the Fine Arts Association had grown increasingly conservative, their stereotyped activities tending only to confirm the provincial character of much of the fine arts in Prague. (As early as the 1860's this unsatisfactory state of affairs had earned well-deserved criticism from the poet, Jan Neruda, and particularly from the painter, Karel Purkyně.)

In the course of the nineties, however, a new generation came to the fore in Czech art. Gathered together in the Mánes Artists Association, founded in 1887, the young artists vowed to overcome the protracted lag in Czech art and, through international cooperation, to help solve the burning issues of European art development. They were dismayed by the poverty and stagnation of Prague's art collections when compared to the purposeful growth and fruitful influence art galleries and museums exercised on the arts in other European cities. Yet the fact was that the Rudolphinum Picture Gallery, as Miloš Jiránek, painter and art critic and the spokesman of his generation, came to realize in 1900, did not possess sufficient strength or even enough will to fill this role. Even less able to remedy the situation were the purely private collections that were accessible to the public only sporadically, for example, the Nostitz Picture Gallery in its Lesser Quarter palace.

In light of the creative upsurge in other areas of Czech culture, the acute shortcomings of modern art collections were particularly conspicuous. The only modern art in the Picture Gallery of the Society of Patriotic Friends of the Arts was a mixed bag of paintings and other works acquired without any set plan or clear-cut criteria, mostly from the annual exhibitions of the Fine Arts Association. These works were usually quite low in quality and had prompted criticism for years. The main schools and leading figures of nineteenth-century European art, with a few isolated exceptions, were not represented at all. Nor was the development of Czech art adequately represented, a failure that more than justified the harsh critical words of Antonín Matějček, a young art historian of the time, who devoted his first monograph to the Rudolphinum Gallery.

Predictably then, artists and art critics embraced the idea of a modern gallery, and in 1901 the joint efforts of artists, journalists, and politicians bore fruit: by decree of Emperor Franz Joseph I, the Modern Gallery of the Kingdom of Bohemia was founded. Headed by an appointed board that included representatives of the arts and of political and public life, the Modern Gallery was divided into two sections, Czech and German. Its first home, in one of the pavilions left from the Jubilee Exhibition of 1891, was supposed to be an emergency solution, but the Modern Gallery stayed there many years. In 1905, the collections were opened to the public. The core of the collections was a retrospective, and in many respects fragmentary, survey of nineteenth-century art, plus some contemporary works.

The year 1918, which saw the unification of the Czech lands with Slovakia in an independent state, was a significant landmark in all spheres of cultural activity. However, the high hopes attending the birth of the republic were not fulfilled as far as fine art was concerned. Disappointingly little was done by the government to help either the Picture Gallery of the Society of Patriotic Friends of the Arts or the Modern Gallery. Nevertheless, it can be said that the republic opened a new era for the Picture Gallery. The credit for this goes to its newly appointed director, Dr. Vincenc Kramář, Franz Wickhoff's pupil and Max Dvořák's friend during his studies in Vienna, an art historian endowed with a penetrating sense of values and a specialist thoroughly familiar with the problems of modern art. Under his guidance, and in conformity with a well-considered program announced in 1921, the Picture Gallery was gradually fashioned into a professionally managed institution. The collections were subjected to expert classification, systematic completion, and scientific treatment, with modern principles of museology applied throughout.

Regrettably, Dr. Kramář's efforts did not receive adequate backing from the state or the public. In the difficult years following World War I, the Rudolphinum, originally dedicated to the arts, was sold by the Bohemian Savings Bank to the state and used to house the National Assembly. As early as 1919, the Picture Gallery was deprived of part of its space; nor were the strong protests by the director and other cultural institutions of any avail when a few years later it was decided gradually to move the collections out of the Rudolphinum altogether. In 1929, the gallery was offered some space in the new building of the Municipal Library (*Městská knihovna*); yet once again what had been envisaged as an emergency measure turned out to be the only possible solution, however inadequate, for many years to come.

The Modern Gallery did not fare any better. It was compelled to stay on in the unsatisfactory Jubilee pavilion, and its program continued to suffer from the conservative ideas of its board. The composition of the gallery's collections and the system used for new acquisitions failed to confront the issues that were gripping the world of modern art. There was a great deal of justifiable criticism; periodicals and even the daily press carried surveys and proposals, and innumerable resolutions were passed by various art associations, notably the Mánes and the Artistic Union *(Umělecká Beseda)*. The only improvement was the gradual and rather substantial enlargement of the retrospective collection of Czech art of the nineteenth century, which was given expert treatment by Dr. Vojtěch Volavka, who was appointed curator of the collection. Despite the fact that outstanding international exhibitions were held in Prague in the 1920's and 1930's, however, the Modern Gallery made no significant acquisitions of German art, which continued as a separate section, or of art works from other European countries. The sole genuine foreign acquisition, of exceptional value, was a fine set of French paintings of the nineteenth and twentieth centuries purchased by the Czechoslovak state authorities in 1923.

A truly eloquent sign of the times is the protracted story of the Modern Gallery's vain efforts to build a home of its own. As early as 1923, a competition was held; the winning design was submitted by Josef Gočár, an architect. In 1927, a foundation stone was laid, but the project ended there. Later on, in 1937, the Picture Gallery of the Society of Patriotic Friends of the Arts was donated to the state, and became the State Collection of Ancient Art. Shortly thereafter, preparations were started for its amalgamation with the Modern Gallery to form one State Gallery. To meet this demand a new and enlarged design was prepared by architect Gočár for a site on Letná, but the fateful events of 1938 to 1939 put a stop to the work already under way.

In the years of the second world war, the State Collection of Ancient Art was directed by Professor Josef Cibulka, an eminent expert in old, particularly medieval art. In a trying and distressing situation, he did a great deal to preserve and protect the collections and to enrich them by a number of significant acquisitions. In 1940, one part of the permanent exhibition was moved to newly altered premises at Zbraslav Castle (King's Hall), which the National Gallery has continued to use for the collection of nineteenth and twentieth-century sculpture. With the rush of oncoming war events, however, all activities were soon discontinued, and the collections had to be taken to a safe place outside the capital.

In 1945, the ancient art and modern art collections were merged into the National Gallery. The single institution was made responsible for works of European and Czech art, both past and present. The subsequent period of revolutionary change made it possible to incorporate in the gallery's holdings significant works from what once were private collections, for example, the Nostitz Picture Gallery in Prague and the Lobkovicz Picture Gallery in Roudnice, plus works acquired through deposits, loans, donations, and the like. In the circumstances, the National Gallery, under the directorship of Dr. Vladimír Novotný, enlarged its holdings in a rather substantial way and at the same time expanded organizationally. Thus a merger of several collections gave rise to the Collection of Graphic Art; the Collection of Czech Sculpture was also gradually completed, while foundations were laid for the Collection of Oriental Art. (For a time, the Museum of Decorative Art was incorporated in the National Gallery; however, in 1969, in accordance with the traditions of the institution, the nature of its collections, and its cultural mission, its former artistic and administrative independence was restored.)

The manifold increase in the National Gallery's holdings called for considerable planning in a number of areas. Most urgent had always been the problem of a permanent site and the need to make the collections accessible to the public. There were several attempts and projects after World War II; yet not even in this period was it found possible to build new quarters for the National Gallery. However, a solution largely in keeping with the character and traditions of the city of Prague was eventually found. The individual permanent collections were placed in historic premises adapted for the purpose; later on similar halls were also found for special exhibitions. Inevitably this disrupted the fundamental unity of the National Gallery system; on the other hand, gaining an expressive milieu was an incontestable asset. The monumentality of the buildings, which were mostly from the Baroque period and unquestionably genuine in style and *ambiance*, combined with an adequate degree of intimacy in the interiors to evoke a harmony of purpose.

The permanent location of the Collection of Old European Art and of the administrative headquarters of the National Gallery is the Šternberk Palace on Hradčany Square *(Hradčanské náměstí)*. 34

An edifice rather lost in the shade of the adjoining Archbishop's Palace, Šternberk Palace stands above the tree-dotted park of the Stag Moat *(Jelení příkop)* and is accessible only by a steep and narrow path; its architectural quality and purity are not revealed until one reaches the courtyard and looks at it from the adjoining garden. The palace was built in the years 1698 to 1708 for Count Václav Vojtěch of Šternberk; architects and builders, in addition to G. B. Alliprandi, included D. Martinelli and Giovanni Aichel-Santini. Painters who decorated some of the halls of the *piano nobile* were M. V. Halbax, Rudolf Bys, and J. V. J. Kratochvíle; the stucco decoration is the work of G. D. Frisoni. The Old European Art exhibits are not extensive, but they are well-balanced. While not equally representative in all aspects, the collection does have a number of outstanding works, and, on the whole, gives an idea of the main European schools of art.

Italian art had always been one of the weak points of the Picture Gallery of the Society of Patriotic Friends of the Arts, though as years went by it was found possible to make it more representative through some acquisitions and loans of significant works from public and church property. The several altars and medium-size panels illustrate modestly but accurately the developmental problems in the *trecento* of several regional schools, particularly the Venetian and the Florentine. Among the most outstanding works are the Altar by Nardo di Cione (associated with the name of Orcagna), the painting by Bernardo Daddi, strong in design and emotionally evocative, and the *Lamentation over Christ* by Lorenzo Monaco, which is expressive and even tragic. The extent and significance of the *quattrocento* are documented by four works only: a single painting by Benozzo Gozzoli and Pasqualino Veneto, a stucco relief from Donatello's workshop, and colored terra cottae by Luca della Robbia. The art of the *cinquecento* is represented by several important works, including a painting in lyrical colors by Palma Vecchio, the portrait of Angelo Bronzino, moderate both as to proportion and color, an exquisitely harmonious painting of the Madonna by Sebastiano del Piombo, and the matured portrait of Lorenzo Lotto. A later stage of development is indicated by the paintings of Domenico Fetti and Jusepe de Rivera, and an integrated impression is created by the group from

the Venetian *settecento* and the paintings by Canaletto, Sebastiano Ricci, G. B. Tiepolo, G. B. Pittoni, and Francesco Guardi.

The Collection of German Art is essentially of an early date, having been assembled gradually in the years following the Picture Gallery's founding. The way fifteenth-century art became differentiated in various regions is covered by only a few paintings in the collection. Truly significant works, like Albrecht Dürer's *Rosary Feast*, created in 1506 during the artist's journey to Italy, are limited to a later period. The Dürer painting was acquired by Rudolph II, and it was the only one of the principal works of his collection that remained permanently in Prague. (It was in the possession of the Strahov Monastery, from which the Czechoslovak government bought it—substantially damaged by damp—in 1932.)

Other works in the German collection are two altar wings in blue grisaille by Hans Holbein the Elder, the moving *Passion of St. Dorothy* by Hans Baldung Grien, and paintings by Bernhard Striegel and H. L. Schäufelein; the artistic work of Lucas Cranach the Elder is richly represented in its full range from sober matter-of-factness to brilliancy of color. Of outstanding quality is one of the paintings by Albrecht Altdorfer, who made dramatic use of both form and color in the cycle *The Legend of St. Florian*. Together, these works constitute a related and integrated survey of the values that are characteristic of the German Renaissance.

As for later periods, the Prague collection can boast of only a few outstanding examples of Austrian and German art. Yet there is enough for the viewer to gain a good idea of the Austrian Baroque and Rococo found in the paintings by Paul Troger, F. A. Maulbertsch, and M. J. Schmidt and the landscape paintings of the two Brands.

The art of the Netherlands' two schools, Flemish and Dutch, which developed independently after the first years, comprise the greatest number of European exhibits. This is a natural outcome of the traditional interest in art shown by the Flemish and the Dutch, and of the large number of their works collected by noblemen and burghers in the eighteenth and nineteenth centuries. The gallery does not have much from the important first period, but in a number of later works the radiant splendor of the "Flemish Primitives" can be appreciated.

The three-piece altar, *Adoration of the Three Magi*, by Geertgen tot Sint Jans is crystallic and fine in both its vision and expression; at the same time it tends to evoke a poetic atmosphere in which here and there one seems to trace echoes of the Symbolist moods of the Maeterlinck generation. Another triptych on an identical theme by Joos van Cleve differs in its preciosity and rather stiff formal features and in its impersonal, even frigid style, which verges on Mannerism.

A major work dating from a watershed between the two development schools (Flemish and Dutch) is the painting of the *Madonna and St. Luke* by Jan Gossaert, nicknamed Mabuse, in which the deliberate tectonic solution is made to harmonize with the sober, lyrically emphasized treatment. (This was originally in St. Rombald's Cathedral in the Flemish town of Mechelen, but from the end of the sixteenth century it decorated the main altar of St. Vitus' Cathedral in Prague Castle.) In a number of paintings, starting with works by Henri met de Bles and Cornelis Massys through those by both Mompers, one can follow the genesis of landscape painting as a genre in its own right and in its gradual emancipation from the fetters of religious, allegorical, and narrative scenes. The supreme work along these lines is *The Haymakers* (1566) by Pieter Brueghel the Elder, the only painting in the cycle *The Seasons* that was to remain in Prague. The breath-taking panoramic landscape, vibrant with the rhythm of human labor, and the fullness and freshness of expression in both material and color make it one of the most valuable works in the National Gallery. The art of Pieter Brueghel the Elder left its mark on the work of his sons, who are quite well represented in the Prague collection.

The characteristic features of Flemish painting —its sensuous fullness and exquisite skill—can be observed in the large painting by Joachim Beuckelaer, in the still lifes by Frans Snyders and Jan Fyt, in the robust brush work of Jacob Jordaens *(Bust of an Apostle)*, and in the large group of paintings by Peter Paul Rubens and his workshop. Rubens' many-sided art is well represented; included are the two large altar paintings made for St. Thomas' Church in Prague (1633–1639), vigorous character portraits, as well as vividly authentic sketches *(Expulsion from Paradise)*. Although the work of Anton van Dyck is not adequately represented in Prague,

the other pole of Flemish painting with its suggestion of intimacy is documented by several first-rate works, for example, the still lifes by Jan Davidsz de Heem, the seascapes by Bonaventura Peeters, and the indoor scenes of David Teniers.

The impression of a really integrated whole is evoked by the group of Dutch paintings, some of which have been part of the collection as far back as the middle of the nineteenth century. The *Portrait of Jasper Schade van Westrum* has all the spontaneity, straightforwardness, moderation, and nobility of the mature art of Frans Hals. Rembrandt's early work is represented by the powerful and perfectly balanced *Scholar at a Table* (sometimes referred to as *The Rabbi*), dating from 1634. The influence exercised by Rembrandt's art over his immediate disciples is seen in *Vertumnus and Pomona*, an artistically and emotionally profound painting by Aert de Gelder, and in the more sophisticated and colder work of Gerbrandt van den Eeckhout and Christopher Paudiss.

The various kinds of Dutch painting of the seventeenth century are evenly represented in the collection: Interior scenes mirror the customs, manners, and way of life of the period (Jacob Ochtervelt, Gerard Ter Borch, Gerrit Dou, Gabriel Metsu, Adriaen van Ostade, Jan Steen, and others); Dutch landscape paintings range from a realistic, matter-of-fact depiction of nature to the cosmic experience of changing clouds, water, and light (Pieter de Molyn, Aert von der Meer, and, in particular, Jan van Goyen and Jacob Ruisdael); finally, the still lifes uncover and depict the physical beauty and poetry hidden in simple, everyday things (Pieter Claesz, Willem Claesz Heda, Willem Kalf, Jan Jansz van de Velde, and others).

Two outstanding paintings of the Spanish school bear witness to its importance in the development of art and to the enthralling mastery of its leading representatives. The subtlety of El Greco's brush successfully conveys the ecstatic exaltation that animates his *Bust of Christ*. The *Portrait of Don Miguel Lardizábal* shows the depth of Francisco Goya's psychological awareness, manifested in the penetrating and finely shaded colors and the free, even dramatic treatment.

The early French school of painting is represented by only a few works by such artists as Pierre Mignard, François Boucher, and Hubert Robert, **36** in contrast to the magnificent collection of French art of the nineteenth and twentieth centuries. Two works by unknown Greco-Egyptian masters of the third century A.D. (referred to as the *Stone Portrait of Fayum*) are a rather isolated phenomenon in the collection. On the other hand, there is a large and interesting set of icons that enables us to trace Byzantine influence in specimens of Russian icon painting within the orbit of the Novgorod and Moscow schools.

The Collection of Gothic Art in Bohemia constitutes the most complete, best integrated, and imposing exposition in the National Gallery.

Since March, 1976, the Collection of Old Bohemian Art has been open to the public in new and spacious premises designed for it in the former St. George's Convent in Prague Castle. The building for the convent, which was founded in 973, was enlarged and reconstructed a number of times in the course of subsequent centuries. After abolition of the convent in 1782 it was used for various purposes and was gradually allowed to deteriorate as the years went by. Under auspices of the Chancellery of the President of the Republic, reconstruction of the convent began in 1963, and by decree of the President it was turned over to the National Gallery in 1969 for the Collection of Old Bohemian Art. Chief architects for the reconstruction project were František Cubr and Josef Pilař, who came up with resourceful architectonic solutions to the demands of modern museology. Development of the arts in Bohemia from the Middle Ages to the close of the eighteenth century unfolds in a sequence of exhibits which impressively reflect the influences that crossed the Czech lands in the Middle Ages and which give due emphasis to leading personalities and works in the various periods.

Now installed in the Šternberk Palace, the Collection of Czech Gothic Painting and Sculpture, which shows the reciprocal influences of the Emperor's Prague Court and the land of Bohemia, richly documents the upsurge of creative work during the reigns of Charles IV and Wenceslas IV; in a continuous row of paintings and sculptures one can follow the genesis and characteristic features of *le Beau Style* (the Beautiful Style).

The present large collection started to be assembled in the second half of the nineteenth century,

and its completion is the result of purposeful and systematic efforts by Vincenc Kramář and the National Gallery's subsequent directors. New insights have been gained owing to the systematic and expert work of restorers—particularly Bohuslav Slánský and, more recently, his pupils—as well as to the scientific and technical work performed by such experts as Antonín Matějček, Albert Kutal, and Jaroslav Pesina. In recent years, new teams of young researchers have produced a large body of information that enables us to evaluate properly this most significant period in the history of art in Bohemia. The results of many years of scientific efforts have not yet been fully applied, however, in the presentation of many of the outstanding works that have been assembled. What is needed is a form of display that (1) informs the viewer where the various exhibits belong in the development of art, (2) clarifies the relationship between painting and sculpture, and (3) provides clues to the solution of problems that are still outstanding.

The fourteenth century is covered in both sculpture and painting. The state of sculpture in the second quarter of the century is illustrated by the Strakonice *Madonna*, rigid and with touches of monumentalism in form; the *Madonna* of Rouchovany, more lyrical in tone and conceptually closer to a relief; and the two unique works of the Master of the Michle *Madonna*, with its firm, vigorous, and highly developed plastic structure and gentle, frail features of sensuous shading and differentiation. Monumental sculpture is represented by the tympanum from the portal of the Cathedral of our Lady of the Snows, the brass equestrian statue of St. George from the courtyard of Prague Castle, and two gargoyles from St. Vitus' Cathedral.

In painting, the most significant work of the period is the cycle of nine tablets that have come down to us from about the year 1350, the work of the Master of the Vyšší Brod Altar painted in all probability for the Cistercian Monastery at Vyšší Brod. Here one can see a magnificent synthesis of domestic Bohemian traditions based on linear features and the tectonic order and spatial interest of Italian art of the day. It was in this period, too, that the most ancient of the Madonnas originated— the *Madonna* of Veveří and the Strahov *Madonna*.

The latter half of the fourteenth century is documented primarily by works of painters. Six panels from the cycle *Christ's Heavenly Hosts* (total: 127 panels) were painted somewhere in the middle of the 1360's for the Chapel of the Holy Cross at Karlštejn Castle by Master Theodorik, the first artist of the period identified by name in several documents in the archives of 1359 to 1368. He is a painter of powerful and original vision, endowed with an admirable sense of how to convey the proportions of the human body and the soft flowing quality of draperies and with a sense of color that is balanced and, at times, even decorative. Master Theodorik's sources and relationships have not yet been clarified conclusively, but it was within the immediate sphere of his influence that about 1360 the large and great-spirited *Crucifixion* of the Emauzy Monastery was created, to be followed some time after the year 1370 by the votive painting of the Archbishop Jan Očko of Vlašim, which provides significant evidence of the maturing interest in individual characteristics, as exemplified by the figures of Emperor Charles IV, his son Wenceslas, and the donor himself.

The most outstanding artist in Czech Gothic painting is the Master of the Třeboň Altar, who is credited with three tablets, painted on both sides, in a larger polyptych, dating from about the year 1380, which may originally have been painted for the Augustinian Monastery of St. Giles at Třeboň. The scenes of Christ on the Mount of Olives, the Entombment, and the Resurrection, as well as the figures of saints on the reverse sides, provide overwhelming evidence of the artist's supreme spiritual and professional confidence. It is thought that the maturity of his style may be due to some inspiration from the French-Flemish school.

It was from the workshop of the Master of the Třeboň Altar that another outstanding painting originated: the Roudnice *Madonna* and *Crucifixion*, now at St. Barbara's Cathedral in Kutná Hora (its original home was the Třeboň Chapel). The painter's conception and emotional accent show some affinity with the *Crucifixion* of Vyšší Brod (before 1400); it is distinguished, however, by extraordinary expressiveness and dramatic pathos.

Sculpture was largely related to architecture in that period, and therefore is primarily identified with Petr Parléř, architect to Charles IV. There are only occasional pieces of sculpture from this period in the National Gallery.

A new stage of development is heralded by the two-part *Epitaph* of Jan of Jeřeň, dated 1395; in the precise linear character, angularity of the draperies, and contrasting colors, one can see points of departure for the Beautiful Style whose development was to be substantially influenced by the Czech lands. Among the significant and lovely Madonna paintings whose form and lyrical charm are characteristic of the period of the Beautiful Style are the *Madonna* of Jindřichův Hradec, the particularly notable *Madonna* of St. Vitus' Cathedral, the *Madonna* of Zlatá Koruna, and the later *Madonna* of Vyšší Brod (about 1420).

In sculpture, the fullness and elaborateness of perception and the poetic quality of formal utterance convincingly express *le Beau Style* in the modified replica of the Krumlov *Madonna* and the statue of St. Peter of Slivice. An outstanding work of the St. Vitus Forge is the tympanum of the north portal of the Church of Our Lady of Týn. The art of the Master of the group that did the *Crucifixion* in the Church of Our Lady of Týn foreshadows the matter-of-factness and structural integration of the next period; an example is the smallish woodcut of St. John the Evangelist. Characteristic of the transition period are the fourteen tablets of the *Capuchin Cycle* (from the Hradčany Monastery, about 1410); here the remnants of the Byzantine prototypes are interwoven with an harmonious application of contemporary models.

The complex and uneven development of art in the first half of the fifteenth century, when the Beautiful Style was fading and new approaches were emerging, is most characteristically demonstrated by the *Crucifixion*, the work of the Master of the Rajhrad Altar and by the six stylistically related tablets of the Altar in St. James' Church *Chrám sv. Jakuba* in Brno. Here, in addition to some traditional concepts, realistic and epic features made their first distinctive appearance in the developed and unfolding narration and in the straightforwardness of the genre. Following the Hussite wars, it took a long time for the former continuity in painting and sculpture to be at least partially reestablished. Late into the fifteenth century one can follow the fading echoes of the traditional domestic conservatism with its rigid notions and dead-end concepts. At the same time, however, new principles and concerns of Late Gothic art, reflecting the strong 38 influence of German and Austrian art, were spreading to Bohemia from the adjoining territories.

At the end of the fifteenth century, Prague once again became an important center of art, although it tended to lose its previous hegemony over the development of art as, with the passing years, distinctive areas of artistic creativity arose in various parts of Bohemia. In addition, many artists tended to stay in one place for short periods of time only. Thus the attribution to a "Czech master" in some of the paintings and sculptures of the day is to be understood only in relation to the locality where the particular work originated and not to the school or place of origin of its creator. The new approach inherent in the natural depiction of figures, interiors, and landscapes is to be seen in the work of the Master of the Altar of St. George, and especially in the six tablets of the altar ordered by Mikuláš Puchner, Grand Master of the Order of the Knights of the Red Cross in Prague, and dated 1482.

In the early years of the sixteenth century, the victorious rise of the early Renaissance is already apparent in works identified with artists of the Late Gothic period, for example, the significant and versatile figure of the Master of the Litoměřice Altar. Sculptural work of the period is dominated by the Master of the relief, *Lament over Christ,* from the Žebrák Castle, an artist with a vivid, even dramatic vision.

In the new exhibition at the former St. George's Convent Bohemian art of the seventeenth and eighteenth centuries is for the first time presented in a full panoramic survey; the wide spaces of the first floor have made it possible to document the logical nexus between pictures and sculptures, as well as between form and color in the architecture of the period.

The art of Mannerism at the Court of Emperor Rudolph, which in many respects suggests the early stages of the Baroque, is represented by several paintings by Bartholomeus Spranger, Hans von Aachen, Josef Heintz, and, most notably, Roelant Savery, whose half-real and half-imagined landscapes are eloquent indications of the refined atmosphere of the time. One of the artists from various countries of Europe who settled for a time in Prague was Adriaen de Vries, whose sculptures are included here.

The art of the Baroque in Bohemia grew and matured at the crossroads of many influences. Many people took part in its development, not infrequently via dramatic and historical events. The National Gallery Baroque collections are above all a review of painting, the beginnings of which are marked by the figure of Karel Škréta, an artist who as a young man was influenced by a number of years spent in Italy and who on his return was very much sought after as a painter of realistic portraits and altar pieces. His work is marked by a generous vision and firm construction, finding expression in circumscribed spaces and in a moderate color scale. J. J. Heintsch, his immediate successor, with his straightforward realism, does not display such an unusual range of creative ability. It was Škréta's mature painting that was used in the nineteenth century as source and criterion for the public's growing awareness of the domestic tradition.

In the latter half of the seventeenth century, new tendencies, accenting emotionally exalted expression, were brought to Bohemia by Michael Willmann, a Silesian painter of the Flemish school. Similarly oriented works by J. K. Liška, his stepson, evince a more sober and constrained note.

The process of differentiation among individual genres at the close of the seventeenth century echoed the diversity of international tastes of the day. Examples are paintings by J. R. Bys, still lifes by J. V. Angermayer, and landscapes by J. J. Hartmann.

In Petr Brandl, the second leading figure of Bohemian Baroque painting, an outstanding artistic personality made his appearance as the seventeenth century gave way to the eighteenth. A great figure, Brandl was the product of his home environment in which various European influences had been assimilated. His evolution can be followed in extensive altar paintings and numerous portraits, in which is found a range of techniques from firmly vaulted columns and clear color chords to loosened and dramatized thick layers of color.

The collection also includes a representative selection of the work of Jan Kupecký, one of the Czech exiles, whose work sprang from Italian roots and matured in Vienna and Nürnberg; his impressive portraits, done in the prevailing international style, testify to the artist's background and to his feeling for psychologically shaded details. V. V. Reiner's work is significant primarily for his ceiling and wall paintings, but there are some live studies, especially landscape paintings, that are evidence of the artist's unusual feeling for color. Elements of the Rococo style influenced by the Venetian school of painting are demonstrated by the paintings of Antonín Kern, a native of north Bohemia, while in the genre paintings of Norbert Grund, the conclusion of a cycle of development is heralded in the fundamental transformation of both structural and conceptual aspects of the artist's expression.

The extent and development of Bohemian Baroque sculpture can be followed today in comparative completeness in the National Gallery collections. Monumental works (in wood as well as stone) and minor and occasional works or sketches bear witness to the way in which creative ideas crystallized. Represented here is the continuity of development, starting with the austere and massive works of J. J. Bendl, moving on to the first impact of Roman influence in the creations of M. V. Jäckl, and then to the more straightforward manner of work of František Preiss, which was based on the native workshop tradition. Several unique works illustrate the art of the master of Baroque, M. B. Braun, who expressed pathos by equally effective use of form and light in dramatizing gesture and drapery.

Equally well presented is F. M. Brokoff, Braun's exact artistic opposite, an artist with a broad sense of tectonics and of monumental accent. Rococo feeling is characteristic of works by K. J. Hiernle, Ignác Weiss, the wood carver, and Lazar Widmann, who was active in west Bohemia. The period is concluded in the second half of the eighteenth century by the works of Ignác Platzer, a classicist, and finally Richard Prachner and his son.

The Collection of Modern Art, including Czech painting and sculpture of the nineteenth and twentieth centuries, has not yet been provided with a worthy home. Parts of individual sections have been placed on view in a number of buildings, or made accessible to the public through occasional short-term exhibitions. Only the Collection of Nineteenth and Twentieth Century French Painting, which is relatively complete, is housed in adequate premises on the ground floor of the Šternberk Palace, and in the adjacent open-air gardens selected works of modern French sculpture can be viewed to advantage.

The collection of French art assembled in the National Gallery since the start of the twentieth century, particularly in the period between the two world wars, and supplemented in recent years, can boast of extraordinary high standards and balance, not only in the succession of exceptional chefs-d'oeuvre but particularly in the continuity and logical sequence of development. The collection starts with a few paintings by Eugène Delacroix, illustrating the extraordinary compass of the artist's creative potentialities, and continues through the landscape paintings of the Barbizon school headed by Camille Corot and Theodore Rousseau, to the grand realism of Gustave Courbet (represented by landscapes as well as by the figure study *Young Ladies on the Bank of the Seine*) and the monumental conceptions of Honoré Daumier *(Family on the Barricades in 1848, The Burden)*. The turning point of the new period is indicated by the noble painting dating from the young days of Edouard Manet *(Portrait of Marcel Proust)*.

All the leading masters of Impressionism are present. There are early paintings by Claude Monet and Alfred Sisley, as well as two landscapes by Camille Pissarro that highlight his stylistic evolution. Auguste Renoir's beautiful large painting, *The Lovers*, is part of the collection; Edgar Degas is represented by the sculpture of a dancer. Three great pictures, a still life, a landscape, and a portrait, present the art of Paul Cézanne. Three oil paintings show the evolution of Paul Gauguin's work from his Brittany period *(Bonjour, Monsieur Gauguin)* to the close of his life in Tahiti. Works of exceptional significance reveal the creative power of Vincent van Gogh *(The Green Rye)*, Henri de Toulouse-Lautrec *(Moulin Rouge)*, Georges Seurat *(Haven at Honfleur)*, and Henri Rousseau *(Self-portrait)*.

The further development of the collection can be traced with equal effectiveness well into the twentieth century through works of the *Fauves* and of artists from the *Nabis* group. Most notable are the works of Pierre Bonnard, Henri Matisse, and Georges Rouault, the more expressive paintings by Maurice Utrillo and Suzanne Valadon, and the landscapes by Maurice Vlaminck and others.

A special place in the Prague National Gallery is occupied by a collection of Cubist paintings, the magnificent legacy of Dr. Vincenc Kramář's private collection. Mostly from Cubism's early analyt- **40** ical stage, they include nineteen paintings by Pablo Picasso, dating for the most part from 1906 to 1913; several later oil paintings illustrate the evolution of the artist's work until 1962. Georges Braque is represented by six still lifes, pleasing in color and in form, dating from 1910 to 1921. A few pictures of unusually high quality also testify to André Derain's role in the heroic phase of Cubism. Among the artists who worked within *l'école de Paris* after the first world war, Marc Chagall and Fernand Léger are best represented.

Unlike the rich and complete collection of French painting, the representation of modern art from other European countries is fragmentary, unselective, and rarely typical. All were acquired as occasional purchases at Fine Arts Association exhibitions or as donations. Nevertheless, the first permanent exhibition of these works has been opened to the public (since May, 1976, in the newly restored halls of Šternberk Palace), and the balanced character and quality of some sections can now be seen. The importance of German and Austrian art of the nineteenth century is illustrated by individual works of C. D. Friedrich, Ch. C. Dahl, C. Spitzweg, F. A. Waldmüller, August Pettenkofen, Anton Romako, and others. Pictures and studies indicating the development of Russian painting toward the close of the nineteenth century are headed by a substantial group of works by, among others, I. J. Repin, J. J. Siskin, V. I. Surikov, I. I. Levitan, and S. A. Korovin.

There are also some noteworthy works in the Collection of European Painting of the Twentieth Century. The decisive influence of Edvard Munch on the development of modern Czech art is evident in two paintings (one of them his *Dancing on the Bank*) purchased from the artist's exhibition in Prague in 1905. There are exceptional works representing modern Austrian painting in the pictures of Gustav Klimt and Egon Schiele and particularly in the comprehensive collection of works by Oskar Kokoschka from 1913 to 1940. The German branch of Impressionist painting can be followed here in individual pictures by Max Liebermann, Lovis Corinth, and Max Slevogt. Expressionism is represented by works of Karl Schmidt-Rotluff and Max Pechstein. Later periods are indicated by the work of Otto Dix and Karl Hofer, and there are two small Expressionist pictures by the young Max

Ernst. Twentieth-century Russia is represented by paintings of F. A. Malyavin and the outstanding works by A. V. Lentulov and R. R. Falk.

The National Gallery has begun only recently to add twentieth-century works of other nations. The Italian school is now represented by several painters, Giorgio de Chirico, Gino Severini, Carlo Carrà, and Renato Guttuso, and the modern Spanish school by Juan Miró, Yves Tanguy, Francisco Borres, Hernando Viñez, and Oscar Dominguez. In this connection, at least mention should be made of the importance of modern Latin American painting as seen in the work of Candido Portinari and Roberto Matta-Echaurren. Work has been in progress in recent years on building a collection of modern art of the socialist countries.

Among the works of European sculpture assembled in the National Gallery, the most significant is the collection of French sculpture of the nineteenth and twentieth centuries. A timely foundation for this collection was provided by the exhibition of the complete *oeuvre* of Auguste Rodin held in Prague in 1902. The gallery has several large Rodin statues as well as a series of portraits and studies. The development of French sculpture can be followed by starting with J. A. Houdon and progressing through François Rude, A. L. Barye, and J. B. Carpeaux to twentieth-century works by E. A. Bourdelle, Aristide Maillol, Charles Despiau, and Henri Laurens. However, other European sculpture is inadequately represented in isolated works by Constantin Meunier, George Minne, Wilhelm Lehmbruck, Georg Kolbe, Anton Hanak, and the Yugoslav sculptor, Ivan Meštrović. The work on supplementing the collection with such new acquisitions as works by Fritz Wotruba, Henry Moore, Giacomo Manzù, Baltasar Lobo, and Dušan Džamonja is a very recent development.

It is only natural that Czech painting should comprise the largest component of the Modern Art collection in the National Gallery. It is relatively complete, especially with regard to the nineteenth-century classical heritage, but regrettably lack of space, for the time being, has prevented the gallery from making it permanently and completely accessible to the public. Nevertheless, a substantial part of the collection can be seen at occasional exhibitions in the Riding School *(Jízdárna)* of Prague Castle. (The Riding School, a Baroque building 41 dating from the end of the seventeenth century, was designed by J. B. Mathey and constructed by J. A. Canevalli; it was restored for the purpose of exhibition by the architect Pavel Janák, in 1949.)

In the development of Czech painting, which in the course of the nineteenth century absorbed—sometimes belatedly—the impulses of European art toward Classicism, Romanticism, and Realism, the works of several artists deserve more than local attention. This can be said of the compelling color work of Josef Navrátil's genre pictures and still lifes, of the poetic vision in Josef Mánes' paintings and drawings, and particularly in Karel Purkyně's striving for structured realism in his still lifes and portraits. In the 1870's this message was heeded by the generation associated with the building and decorating of the National Theater, a group headed by Mikoláš Aleš, a spirited painter and draftsman of lyrical shadings, and by Julius Mařák, a landscape painter of monumental vision. Often, the Neo-Romantic leanings of individuals anticipated some of the concerns that subsequently came to the fore. Adequate space is being made available for a broad survey, in 1979, of the development of classical Bohemian painting, featuring works by prominent Czech artists. The exhibits will be installed on the first floor of the former Convent of the Blessed Agnes (an Early Gothic structure originating about 1230), the reconstruction of which is being completed by the National Gallery.

As Czech art entered the twentieth century, it began a new stage in its development. For the first time, Czech artists participated in the various movements that were tackling the problems of contemporary European art. Impressionism, Symbolism, *Art Nouveau*, as embodied particularly in works by Antonín Slavíček, Jan Preisler, and Alfons Mucha, provided the stimuli for the art of František Kupka, who subsequently, while in Paris in the years 1911–1912, broke with his own generation to become a pioneer of abstract art.

The presentation of twentieth-century Czech painting began with a selection of the most significant of these artists and works crowded onto the third floor of the Municipal Library *(Městská knihovna)* in Dr. Václav Vacek Square. (The library building, designed by František Roith and built in the years 1926–1930, is clumsy in appearance and pedestrian in design.) In the next phase of development, the permanent exhibition is designed to document the contribution of the generation that started to paint before the first world war under the banner of Expressionism and then went on to Cubism—among them Emil Filla, Bohumil Kubišta, and Antonín Procházka. Some artists, like Václav Špála, Josef Čapek, Rudolf Kremlička, and Jan Zrzavý, developed a personal style and perspective. Others, like Václav Rabas, Vlastimil Rada, and Vojtěch Sedláček, turned to the Bohemian landscape.

The development of Czech painting after 1918, differentiated both in concept and execution, was determined by various movements, ranging from the wave of socially involved art of the twenties (Karel Holan, Miloslav Holý, Pravoslav Kotík, and others) to the poetic vision and meditative work of such artists as Josef Šíma.

It was within this circle that the impact of Surrealism was felt in the early thirties. The dramatic events of the period just before World War II were reflected even in their works, as they were in the works of most representatives of Czech culture in those years.

The Collection of Modern Art in the National Gallery also tries, of course, to cover the complex and passionately felt developments in art from 1945 to the present.

The exposition of Czech art has also provided an opportunity to devote appropriate attention to the most outstanding people in modern Slovak art, from Martin Benka through Ludovít Fulla and Cyprián Majerník to artists who began to work after World War II. Collections in the Slovak National Gallery in Bratislava, installed in new exhibition halls in 1976, tell the full story.

In comparison with modern Czech painting, which has failed to find a suitable home for decades and consequently has been seen by the public only sporadically, the collection of nineteenth- and twentieth-century Czech sculpture has been more fortunate. Since 1954, its permanent site, which is indeed adequate, has been the Baroque Castle at Zbraslav nad Vltavou not far from Prague. Built in the years 1709–1732, it is a complex of buildings whose architecture, the work of Giovanni Aichel-Santini, provides generous spaces. The large park has made it possible to let stone and bronze speak in the open air as well. In a new installation in the restored halls and chambers of Zbraslav Castle, opened to the public in June, 1976, the development of sculpture in the Empire and Romantic periods can be clearly followed. After initial stops and starts, that stage, personified by such figures as Václav Prachner, Josef Malinský, and Václav Levý, moved to a firm base in the monumental realism of J. V. Myslbek toward the close of the nineteenth century. In the opening years of the twentieth century, Impressionism, Symbolism, and *Art Nouveau* found expression in the works of František Bílek, Jan Štursa, and others. In the days before World War I, the work of Expressionists like Josef Mařatka, Bohumil Kafka, Otakar Španiel, and others led to Otto Gutfreund, a sculptor with a European reputation, who contributed to Cubism in a creative way.

After 1918, Czech sculpture followed practically the same paths as Czech painting—polarization between realistic, socially inspired creations, exemplified by Karel Pokorný, Jan Lauda, and others, and new imaginative forms found especially in the work of Vincenc Makovský. These two differing approaches serve to guide members of the younger generation in making their contribution to contemporary Czech sculpture.

The third substantial component of the National Gallery is the Collection of Graphic Art, the foundations for which were laid in the nineteenth century, first, by the set of drawings owned by the Picture Gallery of the Society of Patriotic Friends of the Arts and second, by the purchase in 1863 of a large collection of engravings by Václav Hollar. After 1945, these works, plus a number of old and modern graphics, were combined in one collection, which has found a worthy home in the Kinský Palace in the Old Town Square. The building, with its Rococo décor, was built in the years 1755–1765 by Anselmo Luragho to the design of Kilian Ignatius Dientzenhofer, and provides suitable space for rotating exhibitions of items owned by the National Gallery or borrowed from foreign institutions. These exhibitions aim to demonstrate to the public various developmental stages in European and Czech drawing and graphic art from the Middle Ages to the present.

Finally, in 1952, the National Gallery assembled a collection of Oriental art. Based on old and incomplete materials, the collection is being system-

atically supplemented, to as great an extent as possible, with acquisitions from private and public collections. The collection has not yet found a permanent home. Thus it has had to make do with occasional expositions that most frequently focus on ancient Chinese art, in which the collection is strongest. Japanese and Indian art is also partly covered.

In recent years there have been efforts to make accessible to the public at least a substantial part of major collections heretofore shut away in depositories. This determination, coupled with the resolve to extend the National Gallery's activities beyond the capital, has resulted in the decision to install exhibits in some historical sites outside of Prague. Thus, a collection of Late Gothic Czech art has been installed in the impressive setting of medieval Kost Castle in picturesque northeastern Bohemia. Charles' Crown *(Karlova Koruna)* Castle at Chlumec nad Cidlinou, one of the most remarkable structures built by Giovanni Aichel-Santini, has become the site of a survey of Baroque art in Bohemia. Further ventures of a similar character are under way. Outstanding modern sculptors are also permanently accessible now; for example, the work of Karel Dvořák is in Kozel Castle near Plzeň, and the work of Bohumil Kafka is in Pecka Castle near Nová Paka.

During the last few years, in an effort to make the Czech public acquainted with important values in both classical and contemporary art in Europe and other parts of the world, the National Gallery has developed an active program of cooperation with the Regional Galleries, which have been systematically built since 1952 and which have become important centers of cultural activities in the various regions and towns. It has substantially extended its program of exhibitions and expanded its activities involving international cooperation. The renovated Riding School of Valdštejn Palace in the Lesser Quarter is used as a permanent exhibition site. Occasionally Belvedere, the royal summer palace, a charming Renaissance building dating from 1535 to 1563, is lent for exhibition purposes by the President's Chancellery. In addition, as already mentioned, there are exhibitions in Kinský Palace, and smaller groups of individual artists can introduce themselves to the public in the collection of modern art in the Municipal Library. In collaboration with the Museum of the City of Prague, the National Gallery arranges temporary public exhibitions of individual sections of ancient art in the Municipal Library.

Another aim of the National Gallery is to round out its collections through systematic classification and a gradual program of acquisitions. Primary attention is being paid to completing the full range of Bohemian art collections from the Middle Ages to the present day; at the same time, some valuable acquisitions have been made and more systematic efforts initiated to assemble a collection of foreign paintings, sculpture, and graphic art.

The third significant assignment the National Gallery has given itself for the last quarter of the twentieth century is a systematic compilation of its holdings in the form of catalogues which will document the extent of the individual collections, including many interesting works that are not now on display owing to lack of space in permanent exhibition halls.

And finally, the National Gallery's fourth and perhaps most important task is to safeguard and find permanent refuge for all the collections. Additional exhibition space and the construction of modern depositories are both badly needed. This problem is most pressing for the Collection of Modern Art, which has not yet found a worthy and permanent site for its exhibits. However, public response to the National Gallery's various exhibitions, reinforced by Czechoslovakia's present level of culture in fine arts, seems to justify the hope that in coming years, with the participation and assistance of the Ministry of Culture of the Czech Socialist Republic, this task will be successfully accomplished. Then the National Gallery will be in a position to fulfill its mission in upholding tradition and ensuring the cultural development of our own time.

DESCRIPTION OF ILLUSTRATIONS

54 *St. Jerome.* Master Theodorik. Worked 1359-1368 in Prague and Karlštejn Castle as court painter of Charles IV. Tempera on wood. Height 113.5 cm, width 104.5 cm. From Holy Cross Chapel at Karlštejn Castle. Permanent loan to National Gallery since 1959. NG: VO 198

55 *Resurrection.* Master of Třeboň Altar. Worked about 1380 to 1390 in Bohemia. Tempera on wood lined with canvas. Height 132 cm, width 92 cm. From church at Svatá Majdalena near Třeboň, original provenance St. Giles' Church at Třeboň. Acquired 1872. NG: O477

56 *The Haymakers.* Pieter Brueghel the Elder. Born 1525 at Brueghel near Breda, died 1569 in Brussels. Oil on wood. Height 117 cm, width 161 cm. About 1565. Acquired 1946. NG: DO 1956

57 *St. Mary's Square.* Antonín Slavíček. Born 1870 in Prague, died 1910 in Prague. Oil, tempera on canvas. Height 109 cm, width 131 cm. Signed: A. Slavíček 1906. Acquired 1961. NG: O 9012

58 *Dancing on the Bank.* Edvard Munch. Born 1863 at Liten, died 1944 at Ekely near Oslo. Oil on canvas. Height 99.5 cm, width 98.5 cm. Before 1905. Signed: E. Munch. Acquired 1929 from Mánes Artists Association. NG: O 3349

59 *Bonjour, Monsieur Gauguin.* Paul Gauguin. Born 1848 in Paris, died 1903 in Dominique. Oil on canvas. Height 92.5 cm, width 74 cm. 1889. Signed: 89 Bonjour M. Gauguin. Acquired 1937. NG: O 3553

60 *Self-portrait.* Pablo Picasso. Born 1881 at Malaga, died 1973 at Vallauris. Oil on canvas. Height 50 cm, width 46 cm. 1907. Signed on the reverse: Picasso. Acquired 1960 from Dr. Vincenc Kramář's collection. NG: O 8021

61 *On the Otava before a Thunderstorm.* Václav Špála. Born 1885 at Žlunice near Nový Bydžov, died 1946 in Prague. Oil on canvas. Height 82 cm, width 101 cm. Signed: V. Špála 29. Acquired 1959. NG: O 7825

62 *Amorpha. Two-colored Fugue.* František Kupka. Born 1871 at Opočno, died 1957 at Puteaux near Paris. Oil on canvas. Height 211 cm, width 220 cm. 1912. Signed: *Fugue à deux couleurs*, Kupka. Acquired from Prague Castle Gallery 1953. NG: O 5942

63 *Triptych with Madonna on Throne.* Bernardo Daddi. Flourished (under Sienese influence) in the years 1320-1349 in Florence. Tempera on wood. Panel at left: Height 46 cm, width 12 cm. Central part: Height 47.5 cm, width 23.5 cm. Panel at right: Height 44.5 cm, width 12 cm. Early 1340's. Acquired 1939. NG: DO 869

64 *Rosary Feast.* Albrecht Dürer. Born 1471 in Nürnberg, died 1528 in Nürnberg. Tempera on wood. Height 161.5 cm, width 192 cm. 1506. Signed: Exegit quinquemestri spatio Albertus Durer Germanus. M. D. VI. and monogram. From Emperor Rudolph II's collections at Prague Castle, original provenance St. Bartolomeo Church in Venice. Acquired 1933. NG: O 1552

65 *Self-portrait* (Moi-Même, Portrait-Paysage). Henri Rousseau. Born 1844 at Laval, died 1910 in Paris. Oil on canvas. Height 146 cm, width 113 cm. Signed: Henri Rousseau 1890. Acquired 1923. NG: O 3221

66 *St. Nicholas of Rožmberk.* Bohemian master. Sculpture. Lime wood with original polychromy, hollowed at back. About 1380 to 1390. Height 142 cm. Acquired 1950. NG: P 2975

67 *Bust of Christ.* Domenico Theotocopuli (called El Greco).

Born 1541 on Crete, died 1614 in Toledo. Oil on canvas. Height 61 cm, width 46 cm. About 1590. Signed: Doménikos Theotokópulos epoiese. Acquired 1937. NG: DO 234

68 *Madonna and St. Luke.* Jan Gossaert (called Mabuse). Born between 1470 and 1480 at Maubeuge, died between 1533 and 1536 probably at Middelburg. Tempera on wood. Height 230 cm, width 205 cm. About 1513. Signed: Gossaert. From St. Vitus' Cathedral in Prague, original provenance St. Rombald's Cathedral at Mechel. Permanent loan to National Gallery since 1870. NG: O 8756

69 *Portrait of Jasper Schade van Westrum.* Frans Hals the Elder. Born about 1580 in Antwerp, died 1666 in Haarlem. Oil on canvas. Height 80 cm, width 67.5 cm. About 1645. Gift of John II of Liechtenstein 1890. NG: O 638

70 *Vertumnus and Pomona.* Aert de Gelder (Arento de Geldera). Born 1645 in Dordrecht, died 1727 in Dordrecht. Oil on canvas. Height 93.5 cm, width 122 cm. Probably after 1685. Marked with false sign: Rembrandt fe. 1649. Presented by Dr. J. Hoser 1843. NG: O 112

71 *Portrait of Don Miguel de Lardizábal.* Francisco José de Goya y Lucientes. Born 1746 at Fuentetodos, died 1828 in Bordeaux. Oil on canvas. Height 86 cm, width 65 cm. Signed: Fluctibus Rei publicae expulsus pintado p. Goya 1815. Acquired 1937. NG: O 1577

72 *House at Aix.* Paul Cézanne. Born 1839 at Aix-en-Provence, died 1906 at Aix-en-Provence. Oil on canvas. Height 60.5 cm, width 73.5 cm. Before 1885. Acquired 1923. NG: O 3203

73 *St. John the Baptist.* Auguste Rodin. Born 1840 in Paris, died 1917 at Meudon. Sculpture, bronze. Height 199 cm. 1878. Signed: Rodin. Acquired 1925. NG: P 1055

74 *Charles Bridge in Prague.* Oskar Kokoschka. Born at Pöchlarn, lives in Salzburg. Oil on canvas. Height 85 cm, width 120 cm. 1934. Signed: O K. Acquired 1934. NG: O 4459

75 *The Lord's Nativity.* Master of the Vyšší Brod Altar. Worked about 1350 in Bohemia. Tempera on wood lined with canvas. Height 99 cm, width 93.5 cm. From the Cistercian Monastery at Vyšší Brod. Acquired 1949. NG: O 6787

76 *Madonna of St. Vitus' Cathedral.* Bohemian master. Worked about 1400. Tempera on wood lined with canvas. Height 51 cm, width 39.5 cm. Contemporary frame with cut medallions. From St. Vitus' Cathedral in Prague. Acquired 1940. NG: O 8777

77 *Lament over Christ.* Master of relief from Žebrák. Worked in first quarter of 16th century, probably in České Budějovice. Relief, wood. Height 126 cm, width 121 cm. Loan to National Gallery by Museum of the City of Prague since 1957. NG: DP 1196

78 *St. Judah Thaddeus.* Matyáš Bernard Braun. Born 1687 at Oetz in Tirol, died 1738 in Prague. Sculpture, wood lacquered white. Height 192 cm. 1712. From former Jesuit College in Clementinum in Prague, original provenance Church of Virgin Mary na Louži in Prague. Acquired 1939. NG: P 4260

79 *Portrait of Man in White Wig.* Petr Jan Brandl. Born 1668 in Prague, died 1735 at Kutná Hora. Oil on canvas. Height 65 cm, width 50 cm. About 1730. Gift of Bedřich Sylva-Tarouca 1856. NG: O 49

80 *Birth of a Saint.* Karel Škréta. Born about 1610 in Prague, died 1674 in Prague. Oil on canvas. Height 58 cm, width 88 cm. After 1640. Gift of Dr. J. Hoser 1843. NG: O 185

81 *Good Cat with No Sweet Tooth.* Václav Hollar. Born 1607 in Prague, died 1677 in London. Etching. Height 18.2 cm, width 13.1 cm. Signed on lid: V. Hollar fecit 1646. Acquired 1949 from National Museum in Prague. NG: R 86 502

82 *View of Prague.* Václav Hollar. Etching. Height 6 cm, width 9.3 cm. From cycle of *Amoenissimae effigies* ... 1635. Acquired 1949 from National Museum in Prague. NG: R 50 734

83 *Portrait of Wood Carver Vorlíček's Family.* Karel Purkyně. Born 1834 in Wroclaw, died 1868 in Prague. Oil on canvas. Height 140 cm, width 105.5 cm. 1859-1860. Acquired 1924. NG: O 4799

84 *Žalov* (Mourning about Slav hero). Mikoláš Aleš. Born 1852 at Mirotice, died 1913 in Prague. Charcoal drawing on paper. Height 150 cm, width 287.5 cm. Cartoon for part XIV of *Homeland* cycle. Signed: M.A. fecit 1880. Acquired 1948 from exhibits of former Modern Gallery in Prague. NG: K 12 927

85 *Morning Song.* Josef Mánes. Born 1820 in Prague, died 1871 in Prague. Pen drawing on paper. Height 33.4 cm, width 42.8 cm. From the cycle *Musica.* 1856. Acquired 1879. NG: K 147

86 *Black Lake.* Jan Preisler. Born 1872 at Popovice near Beroun, died 1918 in Prague. Oil on canvas. Height 111 cm, width 153 cm. Signed: J. Preisler 1904. Acquired 1945. NG: O 2618

87 *Anxiety.* Otto Gutfreund. Born 1889 at Dvůr Králové, died 1927 in Prague. Sculpture, bronze. Height 148 cm. 1911. Signed: Gutfreund. Former property of Society of Friends of National Gallery in Prague. Acquired 1957. NG: P 4259

88 *Eve.* Jan Štursa. Born 1880 at Nové Město na Moravě, died 1925 in Prague. Sculpture, bronze. Height 190 cm. Signed: Štursa 1909. Original model from which bronze casting was made. Acquired from sculptor's estate in 1927. NG: P 2226

89 *Old Prague Motif.* Bohumil Kubišta. Born 1884 at Vlčkovice near Hradec Králové, died 1918 in Prague. Oil on canvas. Height 98 cm, width 84 cm. 1911. Signed on reverse: Alt-Prager Motiv B. Kubišta. Acquired 1959. NG: O 8189

90 *Landscape.* Josef Šíma. Born 1891 at Jaroměř, died 1971 in Paris. Oil on canvas. Height 80 cm, width 130 cm. Signed: Šíma 1930. Acquired 1960. NG: O 8398

91 *Expulsion from Paradise.* Ludovít Fulla. Born 1902 at Ružomberok, lives at same place. Oil on canvas. Height 91 cm, width 101 cm. Signed: L F 1932. Purchased from artist 1933. NG: O 3439

92 *Madonna of Strakonice.* Bohemian master. Sculpture. Part fir, part lime wood, with carved back, small remains of original polychromy. Height 183 cm. About 1325. Acquired 1924. NG: P 677

93 *Sleeping Boats.* Jan Zrzavý. Born 1890 at Vadín, died 1977 in Prague. Tempera on plywood. Height 78.5 cm, width 106.5 cm. 1935. Signed: Zrzavý 35. Purchased from artist 1935. NG: O 3533

94 *Scholar at a Table* (also known as *The Rabbi*). Rembrandt van Rijn. Born 1606 at Leyden, died 1669 in Amsterdam. Portrait. Oil on canvas. Height 140 cm, width 135 cm. Signed: Rembrandt f. 1634. Acquired 1934. NG: DO 4288

MUSEUM OF DECORATIVE ART

The idea of founding a museum of applied arts in Prague, which originated with Vojta Náprstek, started to take shape in 1867. The efforts of Gottfried Semper and William Morris and the example set by the first Museum of Applied Arts in London inspired widespread recognition of the importance of a similar institution for the Czech lands and Czech arts and crafts. Craftsmen, industrialists, and people in the arts, particularly architects, came to an early agreement on the idea of founding a museum of applied arts as quickly as possible. For a time, while the necessary funds were being raised, they had to make do with a small permanent exhibition of works of decorative art.

The museum itself was not actually established until 1885, when the Chamber of Trade and Commerce in Prague granted the founding charter, which stipulated that the object of the museum—entirely in the spirit of Semper and Morris—was "to awaken by its collections the interest of the public in the artifacts of decorative and industrial arts, to refine public taste, and to stimulate creativity of a finer nature."

In the early years of its existence, this institution acquired temporary space in what is today the House of Artists (originally the Rudolphinum) in Prague. From the outset, the museum held exhibitions and lectures, and the public had access to the library containing every contemporary European book devoted to the history and problems of the decorative and industrial arts. The activities were greatly advanced by Vojtěch Lanna, a collector and eminent art expert, who made part of his own collection available to the museum on loan to enable it to fulfill its charter. Lanna also did a great deal to bring to public attention outstanding works in the various branches of decorative art.

Finally, in 1900, the museum was able to move to its own building, which had been constructed in the immediate vicinity of the Old Jewish Cemetery in the Old Town, not far from the museum's former location. Designed by Josef Schulz, the distinguished Czech architect, the French Neo-Renaissance building was erected in the years 1897 to 1900. The façade is ornamented with figure reliefs representing the individual branches of decorative art in Bohemia and with the coats of arms of towns and cities that had acquired a high reputation for work in the decorative and industrial arts. The reliefs are the work of two Czech sculptors, Bohuslav Schnirch and Antonín Popp. The interior decoration of the building is also connected symbolically with the museum's mission. In the upper reaches of the stairwell are allegorical murals by Ferdinand Herčík, representing six branches of decorative art.

This building, which at the beginning had enough room for all the various departments as well as the library, fully satisfied the needs of that period and enabled the museum to undertake a full program of activities. In accordance with contemporary theory and practice, the museum's holdings were classified into separate, technologically related collections. Exhibitions and lectures were continued. In the years that followed, the museum's collections grew slowly. Under the constraints of very modest financial resources, the museum acquired its new exhibits piecemeal, mostly through donations and bequests.

Activities were not confined to collecting, however. The museum initiated various competitions, with exhibitions of the entries serving to acquaint the public with the latest results of creative work by Czech artists and designers. These activities soon became a potent factor in helping to give guidance and direction to new currents in the field of native decorative art. For example, the exhibition organized by the museum that was based on the achievements of *Artěl*, a vigorous group of Czech artists and designers whose work was destined to become the foundation of modern Czech applied art, gave the Czech public its first opportunity to get to know their work.

The years between the two world wars were difficult for the museum, as they were for all museums of decorative art founded in the second half of the nineteenth century. A change of heart had set in with regard to the mission of such institutions in a society that had adopted a new attitude toward the aesthetics of industrial production. Nevertheless, even in those hard days, the museum found ways to be useful not only to collectors and researchers in the field of decorative art history but also to contemporary Czech and Slovak manufacturers. Industrial design competitions continued to be organized, and, starting in 1921, the museum had the first large-scale exhibitions of Czechoslovak industrial design and work by artist-craftsmen, as well as exhibitions of contemporary foreign work, particularly from Scandinavia. In those years, the museum gave priority to acquiring outstanding examples of historical arts and crafts, although outwardly its full range of activities went on unabated.

Things practically ground to a halt during the years of Nazi occupation. Ideas were restricted, the volume of activities was sharply reduced, and even the building was almost completely closed. The collections were exhibited from time to time in several different locations in Prague, but the only thing allowed to remain in the museum building was the library.

A period of unprecedented development set in after the second world war. The collections were reinstalled, and the museum resumed its regular activities. In 1949, the museum was nationalized; as state property it enjoyed more favorable prospects for future development than ever before. Large state grants made it possible to round out its collections in a rapid and systematic way; as a result the number of exhibits doubled in a few years. Instead of focusing on the collection of glass as heretofore, the museum extended its scope to include ceramics, porcelain, goldsmiths' products, furniture, and textiles, with a view to providing a broad historical survey of arts and crafts.

The large number of exhibits could not be displayed in what was now the narrow confines of the museum building, and the decision was made to build branch museums outside Prague in order to exhibit as much of the collections as possible. For instance, the Museum of Furniture was set up at Lemberk Castle near Jablonné v Podještědí, the Porcelain Museum at Klášterec nad Ohří, followed in recent years by the Exhibition of Furniture and Historical Costumes at the Castle of Hrubý Rohozec, the Exhibition of Baroque Decorative Art at Duchcov Castle, an exhibition of contemporary tapestries in Jindřichův Hradec, and a standing exhibition of the development of lace in Europe in Doudleby Castle. The museum's own exhibitions went on undiminished; of primary importance were those incorporating the results to date of historical research in Czech porcelain, glass, and the like.

From 1959 to 1969, the Museum of Decorative Art was merged with the National Gallery, but in 1970 it was once again made an independent institution, although its structure was modified to meet the demands placed on modern museums. In the Applied Graphic Art section, a collection of art photography is being methodically developed. A new Architecture and Textile Art section has enabled the museum to implement its intensified interest in modern interior architecture, while addressing problems of housing and living conditions. In this respect, it also makes a contribution by giving theoretical and critical aid to present-day applied arts in Czechoslovakia.

Among the museum's collections pride of place is occupied by the collection of glass. From the museum's inception, glass has been the focus of its leaders' interest. The collection is based on a number of gifts of large collections, including an outstanding group of historical glass objects that were originally part of private collections assembled by Vojtěch Lanna, Gustav E. Pazaurek, and Leon Bondy and several sets of modern Czechoslovak glass donated by the Ministry of Culture. These basic collections have gradually been enlarged as a result of purchases, gifts, and bequests, so that to date the glass collection numbers sixteen thousand items and constitutes a record of glass-making from ancient times to the present day. Particularly significant are separate assemblages of Venetian Renaissance glass, Bohemian Baroque glass, and Bohemian glass of the first part of the nineteenth century. Special attention is being given to the collection of twentieth-century glass, to which outstanding works of contemporary, mostly Czech and Slovak, artists are added systematically. To date the twentieth-century collection numbers nearly three thousand items.

In the past, the collection of ceramics was put together with little care or system. Indeed, it has been taking shape through more systematic acquisitions only since the late 1930's. At the present time, thanks chiefly to acquisitions made during the last thirty years, the collection contains groups and specimens of the rarest types of ceramic production, such as Renaissance Italian majolica, German earthenware (stoneware) of the sixteenth century, and seventeenth- and eighteenth-century European faïence. An important section is the set of Bohemian ceramics of the twentieth century, particularly the group that is in the decorative style of Bohemian ceramics of the late nineteenth century and the group of Czechoslovak ceramics up to the present.

For a long time the porcelain collection remained merely an agglomeration of chance acquisitions of European china of the eighteenth century and of Bohemian porcelain objects of the nineteenth century. It was not until 1945 that conditions were finally created for developing this collection, which is today second in size and importance only to the museum's collection of glass. The eighteenth-century collection of Meissen porcelain, the collection of Vienna porcelain from the eighteenth and early nineteenth centuries, and the monumental collection of Bohemian porcelain of the nineteenth and twentieth centuries are the most significant segments. The number of items in the full collection amounts to nearly eight thousand. This size and the sheer range of the contents have made it possible to establish the special Museum of Porcelain at Klášterec nad Ohří, where the manufacture of porcelain in Bohemia is almost fully documented and the supreme period of Bohemian porcelain manufacture, from 1820 to 1855, is impressively represented.

The collection of objects in precious and non-precious metals encompasses specimens of goldsmiths' and enamelers' work; objects worked in pewter, copper, and wrought iron; artistic ironwork; and historical weapons. The collection of gold products comprises two first-rate sets, one of seventeenth-century and eighteenth-century liturgical vessels and the other of jewels in a large collection reflecting the development of jewelry from classical antiquity to the present day. Its most important part is a set of Bohemian jewels dating from the nineteenth century. Fine examples of Czech and Slovak jewelry of the present day also make up a major section.

The museum acquired most of its collection of pewter, in which Bohemian pewter predominates, in its early years. The same is true of its collection of objects in cast iron. A substantial part of the metal collection is made up of Bohemian wrought-iron railings, particularly from the seventeenth and eighteenth centuries. The collection of objects in nonferrous metals is comparatively modest in extent; even so, it does include a number of rare specimens of the foundryman's art, such as Romanesque aquaemanalia and Italian Renaissance door knockers. The collection of cast iron was not developed until after the first great exhibition of Bohemian cast-iron objects in 1933, when the most important specimens were acquired.

In the collection of watches, clocks, and measuring instruments, the most important section is the small group of instruments dating from around the year 1600 and made for the most part by Erasmus Habermel, mechanic to Emperor Rudolph II. The collection of pocket watches gives insight into the development of shape and ornamentation from the second half of the sixteenth century to the present. The largest group covers watches from the seventeenth to the nineteenth century. There is also an extensive collection of table and wall clocks assembled according to the stylistic development of the cases and ornamentation and showing the development of clocks from the Gothic period to the present.

The collection of furniture was assembled very slowly, the reasons being lack of funds and concern about proper storage, since any collection of this kind requires a large amount of space, and space was precisely what the museum now lacked. The actual collection was not undertaken until after the second world war. Then it was gradually put together in such a way as to provide an historical survey of furniture in Europe. The collection is constantly being augmented by new items, including the best works of contemporary Czech and Slovak designers. In addition to fine pieces of European Gothic and Renaissance furniture and of Bohemian furniture of the seventeenth and eighteenth centuries, the group of Czech Cubist furniture from 1908 to 1923 is particularly valuable.

The collection of furniture encompasses wood carvings and small sculpture. Of particular significance is the group of Gothic carved furniture panels acquired in the museum's early years.

The collection of textiles was assembled in accordance with the tastes of nineteenth-century collectors. What had primarily engaged their interest was early textile art—ancient, medieval, and Renaissance. Included in the collection are Coptic dress materials, Italian and Spanish brocades dating from the fifteenth to the seventeenth century, lace, and embroidery. These were followed later by a set of eighteenth-century fans, and finally by specimens of historical costumes, including accessories. This last collection contains a valuable group of fashionable female costumes from the *Art Nouveau* period, unique in number and quality. The best known European centers of tapestry manufacture are represented through several tapestries.

The Museum of Decorative Art in Prague also possesses a small collection of paintings. The portraits are interesting for the knowledge they provide of costumes, the still lifes for historical arts and crafts, and the pictures of interiors for the furnishing to be seen in them. Of major importance is the collection of miniature portraits, which traces the development of Bohemian miniatures in the first half of the nineteenth century and provides documentation for costumes of the period.

The museum also has specimens of craftsmanship in various other materials, such as ivory, mother-of-pearl, and precious stones. Among works in ivory are excellent exhibits of carved household altars in the French Gothic style and sculpture from the Baroque period.

Continuing systematic efforts by the museum's experts have resulted, among other things, in an eminent collection of fine prints documenting typography and illustration and of fine book bindings from the Middle Ages to the present time. It forms part of a collection of works in applied and advertising graphics, which also contains a large set of excellent posters, in which the development of the European artistic poster is documented from its beginnings to the present day. In addition, collections of *ex libris*, ornament patterns, and original designs for various forms of decorative art work have been assembled.

In view of the number and quality of its collections, the Museum of Decorative Art in Prague can be counted among the leading European institutions of its kind. The same applies to its research activities, which cover arts and crafts in all their many forms.

The museum has had the good fortune of always being headed by leading Czech art historians. Of these let us mention its first director, Dr. Karel Chytil, whose absorbing interest was the decorative art of Prague in the time of Rudolph II, and Dr. F. X. Jiřík, whose research interests were extraordinarily wide and encompassed not only Bohemian glass, ceramics, and porcelain, but also Bohemian clocks, and miniature portraits, among others. In addition, both Dr. Karel Herain and Dr. Emanuel Poche have not only devoted their attention to the history of Bohemian arts and crafts, but have also taken a prominent part in the program of theoretical aid afforded contemporary workers in applied arts in Czechoslovakia. At the moment, the museum has a scientific and technical staff of specialists in the areas covered by the various collections. In recent years conservation and restoration workshops have also been set up and systematically expanded.

An important component of the museum is its library, which is open to the public and which can be counted among the largest Czechoslovak libraries specializing in art history. With its individual departments, which conform to the museum's collections, the library serves the public both at home and abroad not only through its regular museum work and occasional exhibitions but also through consultations and diverse activities that make its expertise in the history of handicrafts and applied arts widely available.

95 *Back Cross of Mass Vestment (Chasuble)*. Bohemia. About 1380. Embroidered with gold thread on silk. Pearls, rubies, plate of gold. Height 56 cm, width 25 cm (total dimensions of vestment: Height 130 cm, width 83 cm). Dark-red velvet, fine embroidery in vivid colors, representing Crucifixion. Halos of figures consist of little pearls and rubies, and are trimmed with ribbon of gilded arched plate. Background is partly embroidered with thin gold lace. Formerly in Broumov Monastery in Bohemia, acquired in 1962. Inv. No. 52901

96 *Glass Sculpture*. Czechoslovak Socialist Republic. 1971. Pavel Hlava in collaboration with master glassmaker Stanislav Lenc. Glassworks "Český křištál" (Bohemian Crystal), plant Včelnička. Red glass passing into yellow, blown and hand-molded. Height 40 cm. Spherical sculpture consisting of two parts. Glass cubic plinth joined with sculpture by metal ring. Bought from artist 1972. Inv. No. 75374

97 *Majolica Plate*. With scene of Damocles and Dionysius, the tyrant. Painted with high temperature colors, four yellow lines on reverse of margin. Inscription at bottom: *L'IN-QUIETA VITA AL TYRA DYONYSIO* 1540 and mark. Urbino, Francesco Xanto Avelli of Rovigo, 1540. Purchased 1909 at R. Lepke's in Berlin from Lanna Collection. Inv. No. 11751

98 *Beaker*. Bohemia. Cut by Kašpar Lehmann. Transparent cut glass. Height 24 cm. Signed: C. Leman. 1605. Beaker in tapered form extends on flat stem. In upper section cut allegorical female figures with inscriptions: *Nobilitas, Potestas, Liberalitas*. The figure of *Nobilitas*, seated on throne, bears coat of arms of Wolf Sigmund Losenstein and Susanne Rogendorf, whose marriage took place in 1592. Cut was made after engraving by Jan Sadeler (formerly at Hluboká Castle in sout Bohemia). Inv. No. Z-279/1

99 a *Cabinet*. Prague. Third quarter of 17th century. Colored wood, with inlaid reliefs, black, polished, Cheb work. Height 79 cm, depth 33 cm, length 65 cm. Furniture in prism form with two doors, above and below, with inlaid work in various colors. On outer folding doors, gods Apollo, Mercury, Vulcanus, and figure of Prometheus; on inner drawers, scenes from everyday life; on folding doors of middle niche, figure of Venus. Purchased 1893. Inv. No. 5135

99 b *Detail of Middle Part*

100 *Goblet with Lid*. Bohemia. Early 17th century. Crystal, cut and polished. Height 50 cm. Goblet with lid stands on flat stem, shaft cut in baluster shape, with cut coats of arms of Silesian family of Wimpfen and Bavarian dynasty of Thurn, also framed with two laurel branches, garlands, and crown. Back part of goblet is decked with cut flowers. Purchased at auction in Dorotheum, Vienna, 1908. Inv. No. 10794

101 *Empire Vase*. Slavkov (Schlaggenwald), 1840. Engraved mark: Lippert & Haas at Schlaggenwald 840. Porcelain, painted with vivid colors and gilded. Height 38 cm. Stands on square foot in so-called Medici form. Round shaft, projects in flat stem. Handles bordered with molded masques placed in vaulted part of vessel. Above vaulting, painted landscape from Eger Valley. Foot and vase are painted over with acanthus and palm leaves of gold. Inv. No. Z-L

102 *Bishop's Crosier*. Cheb. 1750. Goldsmith Josef Aycher. Gilded, chased, carved silver, amethysts, painted enamel. Length 154 cm. Fluted straight shaft, knob with inlaid medallion of white enamel with arms of Teplice Monastery and monogram HF AAT 1750 as well as rotunda in which prisoner is being blessed by St. Hroznata (right above him). At beginning of bend, kneeling Pope, on his vestment inscription: Caelestinus III. In bend, Pope seated in front of St. Peter's Cathedral in Rome, to right St. Hroznata and Teplice Church. At end of bend, woman dedicating her child to haloed Virgin. Signed: 1750. Formerly in Teplice Monastery, Bohemia, acquired in 1956. Inv. No. 65038

103 *Minerva*. Dominik Aulíček. Nymphenburg. 1763-1767. China trimmed with vivid colors. Height 37 cm. On base in form of tree trunk, Minerva is seated with her head bent, clothed in ancient, stylized armor. Purchased 1946. Inv. No. 29774

104 *Hyacinth Princess*. Poster. Alfons Mucha. Prague. 1911. Paper, lithography, printed by Václav Neubert, Prague. Publishing house Mojmír Urbánek, Prague. Height 126 cm, width 90 cm. Signed, right below: Mucha. In middle, lady in long robe is seated, her head decorated with crown of stylized hyacinths. Behind her, view toward starry sky is bordered by circular ornamental ribbon with hearts, crowns, hammers, and retorts. Above, inscription: *PRINCEZNA HYACINTA* (Hyacinth Princess). Gift of Publishing House 1911. Inv. No. GP-5176

105 *Tapestry. Pottery*. From *Trades Cycle*. Jindřichův Hradec 1925. Design by František Kysela, produced in Marie Teinitzerová Studio. Wool. Height 270 cm, width 235 cm. Shows potter at work. In front of and behind him two wood shelves with pots and completed tankards. In foreground potter's tools. Near upper and lower edge motifs with twigs and flowers, background and edges unicolored. Acquired in 1925 by Ministry of Culture and Education and since 1961 preserved in Museum of Decorative Art. Inv. No. 59407

106 *Enamel Plate Showing Archangel Michael*. Byzantium, 12th century. Chased and gilded, blue and yellow enameled copper plate. Height 18.8 cm, width 9.2 cm. On golden ground, figure of archangel Michael dressed in tunic with longitudinal stripe decorated with regularly arranged squares. Stripe with similar ornamentation divides garment in middle, thus giving rise to a cross while rest of stripe hangs loosely over left arm. In left hand he holds labrum (flag), right hand is raised. Over right pinion, inscription in Greek characters: OAP, over left: MIXI. From estate of Czech painter Emil Filla. Acquired through donation 1961. Inv. No. 52357

107 *Lead Plaquette*. Prague. Beginning of 17th century. Paulus van Vianen. Chased, chisel-engraved lead. Diameter 16 cm. Signed below in middle: P. D. V. F. (Paulus de Vianen fecit). Round, flat plate, with scene from Greek mythology "Cadmos Kills the Dragon" represented in relief. Plate is framed by shallow laurel wreath. Purchased at R. Lepke's in Berlin

1909. Catalogue No. 321. Originally in Vojtěch Lanna Collection. Inv. No. 11491

108 *Lead Plaquette*. Prague. Beginning of 17th century. Paulus van Vianen. Not signed. Chased, chisel-engraved lead. Diameter 17.5 cm. Round, flat plate with abduction of Europa, sister of Cadmos, represented in relief. Scene is bordered by shallow laurel wreath. Acquired during sale of R. Lepke House in Berlin 1909. Catalogue No. 322. Originally in Vojtěch Lanna Collection Inv. No. 11492

109 *Cash Box with Ivory Relief*. North Italy. First half of 15th century. Studio Baldassar Embriachi. Wood and ivory. Height 19.5 cm, length 21.2 cm, width 14 cm. Prism-shaped little box on pedestal with projecting edge and with roof-shaped lid decorated with frieze with leaf work, upon which winged genii bear vessel and laurel wreath. Side walls are ornamented by relief carvings with biblical subjects, each bordered by one of four archangels. Formerly in Maršov Castle in Bohemia, acquired in 1962. Inv. No. 65 996

110 *Delft Tankard*. Delft. 1679-1691. Lambert Cleffi workshop. Faïence with blue decoration. Height 35 cm. Tankard on octagonal stem with narrow shaft, body in shape of pear, extending toward neck, ending rather high up in beak. Coiled handle. On white, blue flowers and ornaments; in front monogram of Lobkowicz family topped by crown. Part of service manufactured for Václav Ferdinand Lobkowicz. Formerly in Roudnice Castle in Bohemia, acquired in 1950. Inv. No. Z-CCIX/71

111 *Tapestry. New Fabric Hangings with Diana (Detail)*. Paris. 1725 to 1735. Tapestry manufacture, Studio Ovis de la Tour; design Pierre J. Perrot with patterns by P. J. Cazes in cooperation with A. Desportes, painter. Wool. Height 335 cm, width 270 cm. On unicolored ground, composition glorifying Diana. In middle, oval medallion framed by rosary surrounded with garlands of roses and hunting trophies. In medallion, Diana and her train. Under medallion Diana, nymphs, and hounds. Rim imitating carved frame. At corners lilies of the Bourbons in shell-shaped cartouches. Formerly in Horaždovice Castle, acquired in 1950. Inv. No. Z-174/6

MUSEUM OF THE CITY OF PRAGUE

The Museum of the City of Prague, founded in 1883, was the third collection in Prague opened to the public. (The National Museum and the Picture Gallery of the Society of Patriotic Friends of the Arts were the first two.) The city museum's founding was prompted by prevailing enthusiasm for Czech history and by the desire of its founders to promote a better understanding of Prague's importance as the focus of Bohemia's historical development. It arose as a counterbalance to the broader, nation-wide emphasis of the National Museum, and its program was strictly differentiated from the National Museum's.

From the outset the purpose of the Museum of the City of Prague, implicit in the name given the institution, was to document by all available means the history of Prague in all its facets and details. For the National Museum and its program of documenting Czech national history as a whole, Prague was only one of many concerns, one with which the National Museum could never occupy itself as thoroughly and systematically as the Museum of the City of Prague. In spite of its founders' intentions, however, the program laid down for the Museum of the City of Prague was not adhered to in the early stages, when it rather encroached upon the National Museum's sphere of activity. In order to pull the basic collections together as quickly as possible and to open them to the public, the materials collected were not confined to *Pragensia* alone. Thus art works from outside Prague were also collected, not infrequently at German auctions.

Arrangements for presenting the early collections to the public were rather improvised at first. Soon, however, the first installation plan was drawn up, following which thematic exhibitions were installed and the collections arranged in series according to the specialized character of the exhibits. These were supplemented by an Armory and Torture Chamber. The exhibitions were designed to satisfy the romantic inclinations of the time and proved to be very popular.

In the course of the museum's further development, this conception was revised; the objects in the collection were assessed and classified historically, with a view to offering visitors specialized instruction and enlightenment. Prague became the exclusive field for collection, and an appropriate division of labor and thematic specialization between the Museum of the City of Prague and the National Museum was achieved. The former was encouraged to provide documentation on the development of the capital and thus fulfill its original mission. After 1945, the road now embarked upon culminated in the museum's first permanent exhibition on the development of Prague. In subsequent years this exhibition was expanded to include documentation on the city's development to the present day. As a result, after a series of reinstallations, the original romantic approach to the collections was finally abandoned in favor of demonstrating in a continuous series of exhibits what Prague has meant to Czech national life.

Gradually a number of branches and departments was set up, for example, the Prehistoric Department and the Museum of the former quarter *Podskalí,* an ancient and now extinct quarter in Prague. A new type of sculpture exhibition was installed in the fine Baroque interior of Prague's Church of St. Catherine. In 1962, the museum took over the administration of the Prague Loreto, whose world-renowned collection has been installed in the new treasury; the adjoining spaces of the cloister are used for exhibitions.

The museum's program was extended by degrees to include systematic, specialized research in history, history of the arts, and archeology, which led, in turn, to widespread publishing and educational activities, including lectures and special exhibitions.

The present-day activities of the Museum of the City of Prague derive from its original mission, in the sense that anything it undertakes is designed to foster a better understanding of the history of the capital as a social organism. A new and important task is to document the needs and development of the country's capital in today's world. In view of widespread reconstruction and restoration of historical sections of Prague, the museum has undertaken to register changes in the city's physiognomy as they occur. This involves the museum intimately in the process of Prague's current development. Its extensive documentation is not limited to construction. Sound modern theory and methodology have also enabled the museum to assemble a new collection of exhibits in which the changing aspects of life and culture in the city are effectively documented.

The rich collections are what makes it possible for the museum to discharge all its varied duties. Owing to their specific Prague orientation, the exhibits are not duplicated in any other museum in Czechoslovakia. Put together, they give a comprehensive picture of Prague's development in practically every sphere of human activity. The collections assembled by the Museum of the City of Prague show the gradual settlement of the Prague Basin, the emergence and development of its political and social structure, the process of its growth, and the shape of its destiny through its various phases right up to the present day.

The earliest stages of Prague's development are documented through finds turned up in excavations during construction work or brought to the surface by systematic archeological research. As a result, the museum's Prehistoric Department has gathered together evidence of the earliest settlement on Prague territory and of the life and work of its first inhabitants. Rich finds dating from late in the Stone Age constitute the core of the collection. The main objective pursued by the museum's systematic archeological research is to acquire knowledge concerning Slav settlement in the Prague area. The results obtained have served to determine more precisely the relative positions and status of the castle sites in the power structure and organization of Slavonic tribes.

The development of material culture in medieval times is documented by a large collection of artifacts in clay, glass, and metal—the original household equipment of Romanesque and Gothic homes. Their shape and decoration show how prevailing styles in monumental art are reflected in objects of everyday life. Parallel to developing changes in stylistic conception are improvements in the techniques of treating materials and in methods of production; they, in turn, affect the varied forms the handicrafted products take.

In ceramics the stages of development pass from the substantial wide and round shape of the Romanesque through the slim, vertically elongated Gothic vessel, and are completed in the late fifteenth century by the balance between height and width, with the Gothic emphasis on the tectonic structure of the vessel giving way to an attempt to achieve a smooth, soft contour. The basis of the decoration remained the same: engraved or stamped geometrical elements, or motifs, possibly derived directly from the manufacturing process on the potter's wheel. A unique group is formed by vessels decorated with a red line found mostly in central Europe, for example in Germany, in the northern border regions of Bohemia, and in Prague. In addition, the Gothic potter made vessels to meet increased demands for shapes that would fill utilitarian needs: large mugs covered by lids with tall knobs, deep plates with small bottoms and oblique-faced casing, plate-shaped lamps with spouts, and three-sided crucibles. All the shapes of utilitarian ceramics are repeated in miniature decorative pots and jugs, often children's toys, glazed in bright colors and decorated with molded grape-shaped rosettes.

The formal and technical perfection of medieval ceramics is further borne out by fine paving stones and stove tiles, the great number and variety of which lead us to believe that there were large ceramic workshops in the area specializing in baked articles of this kind. Throughout the Middle Ages the decorative relief on the paving stones and tiles has intertwining ornamental and figural motifs. The ornamental designs are represented by a linear intertwined band and a stylized plant-like ornament; the figural decoration, to begin with, has 54 exclusively religious scenes, for example, the Adoration of the Magi, the Lord's Nativity, and the traditional theme of the struggle of St. George and the dragon. In the fifteenth century, a new development set in, leading to the secularization of themes. The reliefs represent scenes from everyday life, with the famous Hussite tiles representing in realistic detail the outfit and weapons of the Hussite warriors.

A special group of clay handicraft objects is made up of statuettes kneaded from light clay or otherwise cast from a mold—figures of the Madonna and Child and of the Child Jesus with various attributes. Sketchily and superficially shaped, these were used either for purposes of worship or as children's toys.

Glass, by virtue of its unique qualities, has from time immemorial tempted man to work it. All that made Bohemian glass famous in its later development is exemplified in the significant find of the oldest existing articles of blown glass on Prague land—two tall, slender cups from a house in the Old Town, dated about the turn of the fourteenth and fifteenth centuries. That they were objects of the greatest luxury at the time of their making is borne out by the fact that they were walled in like real treasure. Such pole-shaped glasses, with the decoration extracted from the glass in the form of little pimples, show how, particularly in glass making, both shape and decoration were derived directly from the structural properties of the material used and from the production process itself in a way that is in keeping with both the aesthetic and practical function of the object.

The collection of medieval products made from metals includes examples of all the handicrafts engaged in metal working. The artistically shaped reliefs on the small surfaces of Romanesque coins bear witness to the high level of Bohemian minting in the early stages of this medieval craft. Metal casting was divided between utilitarian and liturgical utensils. For liturgical objects, special care was devoted to the shaping of the vessel for liturgical ablutions; traditionally, the aquaemanale was in the shape of an animal, stylized and adapted to the vessel's purpose. Products from the medieval blacksmith's forge include a great number of tools for everyday use: examples of locksmiths' workmanship, suits of armor, weapons, and firearms, all showing the punched and embossed decoration and drawing upon the large storehouse of Gothic forms.

The high level of medieval Prague's cultural milieu is evident in the museum's collection of monumental works of Romanesque and Gothic painting and sculpture, which closely track the way the city gradually developed. The most striking find is a set of murals, showing the figures of kings, that was discovered in a house in the Old Town. The set, a rare example of a secular theme in Romanesque painting and one of the most precious monuments of Romanesque Prague, has extraordinary value, as it is the only evidence discovered up to now of the way a burgher's house was decorated in the early Middle Ages.

Freedom of artistic expression and a strong leaning toward realism are the characteristics of a fine example of Romanesque sculpture—the head of a kneeling man in the relief in the Lesser Quarter Bridge Tower, which experts classify as reflecting the influence of sculpture workshops in Regensburg. Sculptural arts in the Early Gothic period are exemplified in the museum collections by the *Madonna* from the Old Town Hall, presumably from the sculpture workshop of Peter Parlř, who is better known for his contribution to the construction of St. Vitus' Cathedral in Prague Castle.

The secularized depiction of the Suffering Christ, showing his tortured face and pierced palms, was adopted by medieval painting and sculpture in the period of transition from classical Gothic to its later phase. *Ecce homo* is the central theme of the mural painting from the burgher's mansion in *Michalská ulice* (Michael Street) in the Old Town and the theme of the wood-carved polychrome statue from the New Town Hall.

The Prague panorama, with the dominant perpendicular of the Castle resting on the footstool of municipal buildings encased in their Gothic walls, had become stabilized in the fifteenth century. It was this that created the preconditions for the city to become an object of artistic treatment in its own right. The first known view of Prague—a woodcut made for Schedel's *World Chronicle*, published in Nürnberg in 1493—marks the beginning of a chronological series of Prague *vedute*. The details they provide of how the city looked make it possible to demonstrate the individual stages in the city's construction and the changes in its architectural styles. Thus the *vedute* become today a valuable source, throwing light on the topography of Prague and frequently serving as an auxiliary guide for the reconstruction and restoration of parts of the city.

With the changing views on style, the concept of the cityscape changed, too, although it remained rooted in an architectonic panorama characteristic of Prague from the beginning. The vistas of Prague in the late 1500's and early 1600's, done for the most part by Dutch artists employed at the Court of Emperor Rudolph II, already show all the signs of the mature Renaissance *veduta*, particularly in the composition of the view and in the accomplished techniques used in reproduction (mainly copper engraving).

A unique work of art among the predominantly graphic drawings is the medium-size oil painting by Lukas Valckenborch, a Dutch painter, which provides unusual insight into a painter's conception of the panorama of Prague in the early stages of this genre's development. In the pen-and-ink drawings of Roelant Savery, the nooks and corners of Prague make their appearance, alongside the familiar vistas of the city. Savery's cityscape discarded the remains of the medieval pattern, with its emphasis on the panorama as the dominant feature, and focused on the foreground as the scene of action. The last Renaissance panorama of Prague that is known was created by Václav Hollar in 1636. The composition of the *veduta* is entirely new here, with the realistic architecture of the city full of space and air. Among the most significant works of this famous Czech engraver are his minute etchings, which are fine miniature drawings of sections of the city, in perfect perspective, showing the river, bridge, and embankment buildings.

An integral part of artistic production in Prague at the beginning of the seventeenth century was the extensive sculptural work of Adriaen de Vries. Much of his work was plundered during the Thirty Years War. The only survivor is a bronze statue of Hercules once part of a group of large sculptures for the garden of Valdštejn's Prague residence.

In the collections of the Museum of the City of Prague, the most significant evidence of the artistically expressive Baroque period is found in the works of several sculptors. The large set of Baroque wood sculptures by Jan Jiří Bendl, the founder of Prague Baroque sculpture, represents the initial stage of the period. Bendl was followed by the serious realism of the famous sculptor F. M. Brokoff and the dramatic statues from the High Baroque of M. B. Braun, which are free of the restraint imposed by the bulk of the material used and, instead, are controlled by the movement of the body and the garment. Also represented are minute decorative Rococo sculptures and pieces in the tranquil classical mold, especially the works of I. F. Platzer.

The collection, however, does not revolve around artists with famous names. Instead, the museum has assembled a large number of exhibits which provide excellent documentation of the original Baroque interiors of Prague churches and the sculptural decorations of burghers' houses. At the same time, the exhibits constitute a valuable source for the iconography of Baroque art. The bearers of Baroque pathos—or possibly of Early Rococo sentiment—ate primarily the motif of *Pietà* and the physiognomy of the martyred Christ emphasizing his human substance and face in the sense of *Ecce homo*.

Artistically, the Prague Baroque *veduta* of the seventeenth century is not equal in significance to its Renaissance counterpart. Thus the 1680 panorama by Ouden-Allen, engraved by Conrad Decker and published in Vienna in 1685, is of topographical rather than artistic significance. This is due to the conservative design of the vista; too, the distortion in scale is in direct proportion to the artist's endeavor to crowd the appropriate number of houses into the given space. A clear-cut artistic conception was not reached by the conservative cityscape of the eighteenth century until Filip and František Heger created their classical, colored copper engravings of Prague, in which they succeeded in conveying the city's *ambiance* in the years 1792 to 1796. A valuable aid to the study of Baroque Prague's topography is a large-scale plan of the city, enclosed by the Baroque fortifications, drawn in geometric perspective by Josef Daniel Huber in 1769.

The appearance of Prague in the 1830's is borne out by an exhibit that is more informative than the *vedute* or even Huber's plan. This is the only preserved model of the city of Prague, made by Antonín Langweil; it shows the historic core of 56

Prague as still an essentially Baroque formation, untouched by demolitions. The conception of a cityscape in the nineteenth century was affected by the contemporary outlook on landscape painting cultivated at the newly founded Academy of Painting in Prague, particularly the way the rigid features of the existing architectonic cityscape were enveloped in rich, luscious vegetation. The best known cityscape painter of nineteenth-century Prague was Vincenc Morstadt, who, in a series of vistas, captured the face of the city with unparalleled precision. By their affinity to landscape painting and the idyllic nature of the figural motifs, Morstadt's vistas are exemplars of the period's romanticism as expressed through graphic art.

An equally important source of our knowledge of life in the nineteenth century is formed by portraits, the most competent of which were executed by Antonín Machek, the greatest creative personality in this field.

Among the items of eighteenth-century craftsmanship that form part of the museum's collections of sets of furniture, clocks, silver, and glass from burghers' houses, the most important is earthenware, which demonstrates a preliminary stage in the process leading to Prague porcelain.

The rich collection of Prague porcelain, of utility crockery of all kinds as well as figural sculptures, bears witness to the rapid development of the Prague porcelain works, which in a few years had evolved from the original small shop to a large factory containing all the equipment of a sizable industrial enterprise. Further evidence of the eminence to which the graphic arts had risen in the extraordinary upsurge of the 1850's and 1860's is the painted calendar plate for the Astronomical Clock of the Old Town Hall by Josef Mánes and the designs submitted for the contest on the artistic decoration of the National Theater.

As regards the end of the nineteenth century and the first half of the twentieth century, the number of three-dimensional museum exhibits has decreased, while photographic documentary records have increased. The Prague scene of those years is also documented in paintings, particularly those by Jan Minařík. His vistas of Prague express the growing interest in picturing the vanishing city, devastated by demolitions at the turn of the nineteenth and twentieth centuries. Political and social contradictions and the consequences of the economic crisis of the twenties and thirties are reflected in paintings by such contemporary artists as M. Holý, J. Rambousek, and K. Štika, whose works were strongly influenced by the antimilitary and social poetry of the years following World War I.

A special collection, the richest of its kind anywhere, is a group of exhibits recalling Prague's craft guilds. The collection exemplifies the specific attributes of the individual crafts and furnishes eloquent evidence of the high quality of the workmanship of Prague artisans and workers from the beginning of the fifteenth century to the abolition of the guild structure in 1859. Excellent guides to the guilds are the sealing sticks, which carry the emblem of the particular craft, and guild strong boxes, through whose shapes can be traced the transformations in style, ranging from the New Town butcher chests ringed with iron bands and dating from the end of the fifteenth century, through the chests with fine intarsia designs from the end of the sixteenth century, to the richly decorated guild strong boxes of the eighteenth.

Guild banners, ranging from varied butchers' banners to the standardized banners made for the coronation of Leopold II in 1791, were designed exclusively to identify the individual guild. An important place in the museum's collection is also occupied by signboards with the guilds' coats of arms, and case coats of arms intended to decorate and mark the seat of the guild, as, for instance, the coats of arms of potters and stovemakers, the center of which is formed by a colored tile depicting a scene from the legendary Fall of Man or the unique coat of arms of the hatters' guild in the form of a glazed case containing miniature hats, dating from the early nineteenth century.

Among the numerous specimens of guild pottery, the visitor's interest is attracted by the huge can of the brewers' guild of 1688, with cut decoration, and the shoemakers' can in the shape of a riding boot, while among the exhibits related to religious rites are funeral emblems intended to decorate the catafalque of the deceased member of the particular guild.

This survey of the main collections assembled by the Museum of the City of Prague makes clear their documentary character and significance. The aim has been to assemble as completely and broadly as 57 possible documentary material for the full range of human activity in the area Prague covers. In that way, the museum hopes to make its permanent collections into a first-rate source of historical information about life as it occurred in the center of Czechoslovakia, from the city's earliest days to the present.

DESCRIPTION OF ILLUSTRATIONS

112 *Man's Head.* From relief in Bridge Tower of Charles Bridge in Lesser Quarter of Prague. Sandstone. Height 28 cm. About 1170. Acquired 1893. Inv. No. 9 009

113 *Miniature Figurines.* Prague. 15th to 16th century. Unglazed clay. Height of tallest figure 12.5 cm. Discovered in Old Town during excavation works
a *Madonna and Child.* 15th century. Inv. No. 17 570
b *Angel.* 15th century. Inv. No. 17 566
c *Tiny Horse.* 16th century. Inv. No. 1 140
d *Woman in Secular Costume.* 15th century. Inv. No. 17 646

114 *Cup.* Discovered in house No. 692 in Old Town of Prague. Glass. Height 43 cm. About 1400. Acquired 1899. Inv. No. 11 862

115 *Guild Burial Coat of Arms.* Prague. 1591. Embroidery on black velvet. Diameter 43 cm. Formerly property of Shoemakers Guild in Lesser Quarter and in Hradčany (Prague). Acquired 1911. Inv. No. 33 863/2

116 *Guild Signboard of Potters and Tilers.* About 1530. Color-glazed ceramic in wooden chest with movable wings. Height 88 cm, width of closed signboard 55 cm. Acquired 1926. Inv. No. 34 262

117 *Guild Box of Cloth Cutters and Clothiers.* Prague. 1609. Inlaid wood, polychrome reliefs. Height 47.8 cm (with lid), width 58.7 cm, depth 39.3 cm. Acquired 1893. Inv. No. 8 780

118 *Guild Jug of Shoemakers in Prague.* Prague. 1715. Pewter. Height 73 cm. Acquired 1911. Inv. No. 33 869

119 *Head of John the Baptist.* Bohemian master. About 1510-1520. Wood. Height 31 cm. Inv. No. 17 305

120 *Hercules with Apples of Hesperides.* Adriaen de Vries. Born about 1560 in the Hague, died 1626 in Prague. Bronze. Height 162.5 cm. After 1620. From house No. 559 in Old Town of Prague. Acquired 1905. Inv. No. 14 576

121 *St. Ignatius' Group.* Ferdinand Maximilián Brokoff. Born 1688 at Červený Hrádek, died 1731 in Prague. Linden wood, polychrome. Height 80 cm. Before 1711. Model of statuary for Charles Bridge, Prague. Acquired 1896. Inv. No. 10 796

122 *Beaker with View of St. Vitus' Cathedral.* Antonín Kothgaser. Born 1796 in Vienna, died 1851 in Vienna. Painting on transparent glass, cut and etched ornament. Height 12.2 cm. About 1825. Acquired 1943. Inv. No. 41 338

123 *Chalice.* Bohemia. 1510. Gilded silver, enamel, semiprecious stones. Height 24.5 cm. Gift of Kryštof Ferdinand Popel of Lobkowicz (died 1658) to Prague Loreto. Inv. No. Loreto P-69

124 *Diamond Monstrance.* Jan B. Känischbauer. Born 1668 in Anger, died 1739 in Vienna. Matyáš Stegner. Gilded silver, enamel, 6,222 diamonds. Height 89.5 cm. Vienna. 1696-1699. Foot of monstrance contains following engraved inscription: "Durch Matthias Stegner und Johann Känischbauern. Inventiert und gemacht Inn Wienn 1699." Made for Prague Loreto on commission of Eva Ludmila Františka, Countess of Kolovrat. Inv. No. Loreto P-300

TREASURY OF ST. VITUS' CATHEDRAL

Because of its size and its great artistic and historical value, the treasury of St. Vitus' Cathedral is one of the major collections of goldsmiths' art in the Czechoslovak Socialist Republic.

The most significant items are those that date from the days of Emperor Charles IV and some that appear in records as far back as the eleventh century. A lover of works made of gold and precious stones and an eager collector of religious relics, Charles started rearranging and augmenting the St. Vitus ecclesiastical treasures as early as 1344 when the Gothic cathedral was founded.

A chronicle from the year 1069 records the fact that since the early Middle Ages church treasures were kept in a special chamber of the ancient Romanesque basilica of St. Vitus. Among the early items that have been preserved are the helmet and byrnie of St. Wenceslas, one early feudal sword, and the shrine of Limoges.

The Emperor used the existing treasury of liturgical vessels as the foundation on which he systematically enlarged the collection according to his own tastes and interests. Special closets were built in the new cathedral above St. Michael's Chapel (the vestry) and in the chapel dedicated to St. Wenceslas, the Emperor's patron saint. Chapels and closets served as depositories for the old and new treasures.

Later, the St. Vitus' Cathedral Chapter was entrusted with maintaining the treasury. Starting in 1354, the individual items were entered in inventories, six books of which dating from the fourteenth century have been preserved. The Emperor established a Court workshop for the execution of orders for objects in gold and precious stones. Peter Parlř, the Court architect and sculptor, had artistic responsibility for the work, but organizationally, the workshop was affiliated with the Fraternity of Old Town Goldsmiths, founded as early as 1324.

The precious pieces incorporated into the treasury by Charles IV included items he brought with him from the Royal Court of France, where he had spent his childhood, and works of art from the dowries of his four wives. Most, however, were the numerous gifts presented to him by ecclesiastical figures and feudal lords from practically all of Europe. Thus it happened that during his rule, which lasted until 1378, one of the most important cathedral treasuries in the world of that time came into being in Prague. According to one of the inventory books, it comprised about 750 items, including goldsmiths' works, silk cloths, embroidered liturgical garments, and illuminated manuscripts.

One of the Emperor's additions was the Royal Crown of Bohemia, which Charles IV had newly made of pure gold, decorated with 91 precious stones and 20 pearls in 1346. Later, it was placed on the gold reliquary bust of St. Wenceslas, which Charles ordered before 1358. The cathedral treasury also included St. Wenceslas' Tomb (1358), which was installed in the chapel dedicated to the saint on the cathedral's gallery. Artistically incorporated into the costly wall decorations of the chapel, the *tumba* (tomb) was covered with panels of gold and silver, others with chased reliefs, and one hung with 37 ancient cameos, 935 precious stones, and 448 pearls, while in front was a gold statue of St. Wenceslas.

The two pieces honoring the nation's patron saint were outstanding specimens of the jeweler's art. Goldsmiths' works in the treasury included 13 statues of saints embossed in silver and 27 gold and silver reliquaries. Regrettably, none of these has been preserved with the exception of the Crown of St. Wenceslas, which was protected from despoliation by its political and symbolic significance. Nor were most of the other items in the remaining Charles inventory saved. In fact, the only other pieces that survived the Hussite period were those in the care of Prague archbishops at their country seats, for example, the Bohemian Coronation Cross and the golden cross of Pope Urban V.

The man who did the heaviest damage to the treasury was Charles' second son, Sigismund, who, in 1420 and 1421, had much of the goldsmiths' and silversmiths' work moved to the castles of Karlštejn and Oybin where they were used mainly to provide pay for imperial mercenaries. When the treasury reverted to St. Vitus' Cathedral in 1435, it consisted of hardly anything but insignificant remains.

However, new patrons of the arts came forward to fill some of the gaps. Among them were Canon Václav of Krumlov, Hanuš of Kolovrat, and subsequently the new Catholic King Vladislav, of the Polish House of Jagellon, to whom the treasury is indebted for three masterpieces—the busts of St. Wenceslas, St. Adalbert, and St. Vitus, ascribed to Václav of Budějovice, the Court goldsmith. The King's example found its imitators, as evidenced by the great number of Late Gothic goldsmiths' works that have been preserved.

The first Hapsburgs on the Czech throne left no particular trace on the treasury, however. Only Rudolph II is credited with significant and memorable items, for example, the cross of Archbishop Medek with its admirably modeled corpus and the Lobkowicz Plenary (Mass book), engraved from a design unmistakably by J. Sadeler. In 1645, the treasury was enlarged by the addition of remnants of the Karlštejn Castle treasury founded by Charles IV. It was then that such works of art as the two early medieval *olyphantes*, the French Gothic ivory statuette of the Virgin Mary, the Augsburg silver bust of St. Anna, Mary, and the Child, and others were added.

At the same time, recatholicization of Bohemia after the defeat of the uprising of the Estates against the Hapsburgs was reflected in a new expansion of the Cathedral treasury. Contributions by feudal lords after the Battle of White Mountain were prompted by the urge to outdo one another as well as by

the genuine piety of some. New development of the goldsmiths' craft—in the seventeenth and eighteenth centuries, the goldsmiths were concentrated predominantly in the Lesser Quarter, just below Prague Castle, in the workshops of M. Hrabek, L. Lichtenmschopf, and C. Gschwander—resulted from the aristocracy's patronage, and the treasury was filled with magnificent monstrances, chalices, and other liturgical items. Following the signs and dates on these articles, one can trace from their form and ornamentation the evolution of styles from early Baroque to Rococo in the latter part of the eighteenth century. The artistic legacy of the period culminates in four embossed silver busts of patron saints of Bohemia, worked by R. Ranzoni and made at the expense of Archbishop Breuner, silver candlesticks, a precious can, and a lavabo, all dating from 1699.

After 1780, when numerous religious orders were abolished and their property secularized by Joseph II, the treasury acquired at little cost a number of valuable works of goldsmiths' High Gothic art from the abolished Georgian Convent and liturgical vestments from other convents. Unfortunately, they were only meager compensation for the losses incurred at the beginning of the fifteenth century. And not long afterward, in Napoleonic times, financial needs of the Vienna state exchequer resulted in another reduction of the cathedral treasury, which was deprived of some noteworthy medieval and contemporary items, including two silver busts. Only Emperor Francis I's personal intervention made it possible to preserve the Baroque silver sarcophagus, executed by the Vienna artist, Joseph Würth, from a design by Joseph Emanuel Fischer of Erlach. To this day it is the showpiece of the Prague cathedral. As before, later gifts, like the precious French monstrance donated by the *émigré* King Charles X in 1830 or the golden rose, a papal gift transferred to the treasury by the former Empress Marie Anne, could not make up for the losses suffered in the Napoleonic Wars.

The most recent acquisition of note, brought to the St. Vitus' Cathedral treasury in 1950 from the evacuated Cistercian Monastery at Vyšší Brod, is the Záviš Cross. The cross is a remarkable synthesis of west European goldsmiths' art of the thirteenth century and Byzantine art of enameling dating from the eleventh and twelfth centuries.

So reads the almost thousand-year history of the treasury of St. Vitus' Cathedral. In appreciation of its historical significance and artistic value, it has been moved from the narrow and dark vaults of the cathedral to the light and spacious interior of the Chapel of the Holy Cross in Prague Castle's second courtyard. In 1963, it was reinstalled, and in 1966 it was catalogued by the present writer.

DESCRIPTION OF ILLUSTRATIONS

125 *Coronation Jewels of Kingdom of Bohemia.*
a *Crown of St. Wenceslas.* Prague. 1346. Gold, 91 spinels, sapphires, emeralds, and one ruby, Byzantine cameo with Crucifixion dating from 13th century, and 20 pearls. Height 19 cm
b *Apple.* Prague. About 1605. Court workshop of Rudolph II. Gold with embossed scenes from Old Testament. Precious stones, pearls, enamel. Height 22 cm
c *Scepter.* Prague. About 1605. Court workshop of Rudolph II. Gold, precious stones, pearls, enamel. Length 67 cm

126 *Reliquary Cross of Pope Urban V.* Rome or Prague. About 1375. Perhaps by Court goldsmith Hanuš. Silver stem. Late Gothic (1522). Gold with engraved nielloed drawings, sapphires, and spinels. Above: Calvary. On left: Pope Urban and Cardinal Belfort. On right: Charles IV and Wenceslas IV. Below: Pope Urban handing over a relic of Christ's veil to Charles IV. Height 57 cm

127 *Reliquary of St. Nicholas.* Venice. First half of 13th century. Stem, gilded silver, decorated with gems in Prague, bears alabaster receptacle containing relic of saint's finger. Height 21 cm.

128 *Zdviš Cross.* Upper part: Hungary. First half of 13th century. Gold, filigree, precious stones, and cloisonné enamel medallions with figures of Apostles and angels. Enamels: Byzantium, 11th to 12th century. Gilded silver stem. Mid-19th century. Height 80 cm. Gift of Záviš of Falkenstein to Cistercian Monastery in Vyšší Brod about 1280. Added to St. Vitus' Treasury in 1950

129 *Reliquary Bust of St. Ludmila.* Bohemia. Mid-14th century. Probably workshop of Benedictine Monastery at Břevnov. Silver, embossed and gilded. Height 34 cm. Purchased at time of the disbandment of St. George's Convent to form part of St. Vitus Treasury in 1782

130 *Relic Can.* Prague. 1348. Crystal: South Italy. 12th to 13th century. Lid: Prague. First half of 16th century. Cut crystal, embedded in gilded silver mounting, stem decorated with precious stones. Height 40 cm. Relic (presumably table cloth of Last Supper) preserved in can. Gift of Ludwig, King of Hungary, to Charles IV. 1348

131 *Reliquary Bust of St. Vojtěch.* Prague. About 1486. Workshop of goldsmith Václav of Budějovice. Silver, embossed and gilded. Height 52 cm. Gift of Vladislav the Jagellon for St. Vitus' Cathedral Treasury

132 *Ivory Horn (Olyphant).* South Italy. 11th century. Sicilian-Arabic work. Ivory, carved into rings depicting hunting scenes. Length 55 cm

133 *Helmet of St. Wenceslas.* Western Europe. 9th century. Subsequent decoration of nosepiece and border. Bohemia, 12th century. Forged iron, partly silver coated. Height 24 cm

134 *Pearl embroidery on cloth.* Prague. Second half of 14th century. Painted faces: 17th century. Busts of Christ, St. Wenceslas, and St. Vitus. Height 22 cm, width 40 cm

135 *Coronation Cross with Relics of Martyrdom of Christ.* France. 13th century. Modified by order of Charles IV into relic cross and decorated. Stem, gilded silver, of 1522. Gold, crystal, sapphires, ancient and Byzantine cameos. Height 89.7 cm

PRAGUE CASTLE GALLERY

The Gallery at Prague Castle is one of the newest collections of art in Prague. It is also one of the oldest. It is new in form and museological concept, but old in its history and in the origin of the most significant works. The present collection is made up of valuable paintings preserved at Prague Castle from the rich stores of art works originally assembled at the former royal and imperial residence. It is installed in several Castle chambers, its core being in the Royal Stables of Emperor Ferdinand I (after 1534) and Emperor Rudolph II (1595).

Until recently opinion was widespread that, aside from the few known exceptions deposited in the National Gallery, the outstanding works in what used to be the Castle Picture Gallery in the seventeenth century were irretrievably lost to Prague. However, an investigation by the present author, an art historian, in the years 1962 to 1964 revealed this conclusion to be incorrect and due to insufficient knowledge about what happened to the collection. It is particularly noteworthy that no scientific attention had been given to the old paintings that were still at Prague Castle in more recent times. Many of them are indeed less interesting works of later origin, but in warehouses and other locations not usually accessible to the public a number of remarkable paintings has been preserved, paintings that were part of the Castle Picture Gallery collection as early as the seventeenth and eighteenth centuries. These precious pieces were not really lost; through a quirk of history, their value as works of art, the names of their creators, and their relationship to the once famous collection became obscured by the nineteenth century and, in several instances, even by the eighteenth century. In the thorough investigation of the 1960's, these works were identified and professionally evaluated, and proper

attribution was made. Thanks to the interest in these new findings shown by the President's Chancellery and with the cooperation of the Czechoslovak Academy of Sciences, the present Gallery at Prague Castle was authorized in 1964 as a permanent exhibition; it opened on January 15, 1965. In addition to making valuable works of art accessible to the public, the gallery's collection comprises a documented history that serves to recall the glorious past and the rich abundance of art collections at Prague Castle.

The most valuable unidentified works had reached Prague Castle shortly after the middle of the seventeenth century, probably in the years 1655 and 1656. At that time a new gallery was founded at the Castle to replace the Rudolphine art treasures that had been carried off by the Swedes in 1648 and some that had been transferred to Vienna even earlier. The reason such an extensive collection of about 550 paintings could be built up so rapidly was that Archduke Leopold Wilhelm, Emperor Ferdinand III's brother, Governor of the Netherlands and, prior to that, of Bohemia, who made the purchases for Prague Castle, seized an unusually favorable opportunity, namely the sale and auction of English collections shortly after the English Bourgeois Revolution. Leopold Wilhelm acquired the most valuable part of his own gallery, which subsequently became the Imperial Gallery in Vienna, through the purchase of the Gallery of the Duke of Hamilton. However, the most significant paintings for the Prague collection, about one hundred works, were bought at the auction of the Buckingham Collection in Antwerp in the years 1648–1649.

The seventeenth-century Picture Gallery reflected the tastes and collecting interests of the day. It primarily had paintings from the sixteenth and early seventeenth centuries, with a smaller number from the fifteenth century. There was art of the Netherlands and Germany, but Italian art predominated. Among those best represented were the Venetians, with a large number of works by Titian, Veronese, Tintoretto, and members of the Bassano family. The Mannerism of Florence and Parma was better represented in works by Andrea del Sarto and G. Parmigianino than was the Florentine and Roman Renaissance. Roman Baroque appeared in the paintings of such artists as Gentileschi and Manfredi, masters of the *chiaroscuro* identified with Caravaggio, and the Bologna school could be studied in a valuable collection of works by Guido Reni. Representatives of the other Italian schools could also be found—Strozzi of Genoa, Furini of Florence, Ribera, and Preti of the Neapolitan school. Prague possessed the largest and finest collection north of the Alps of the paintings of Domenico Fetti, who lived in Mantua and worked in the Neo-Venetian style.

The art of the Netherlands was also well represented, starting with older masters, such as Geertgen tot Sint Jans and Joos van Cleve. Various genres were represented by the classical works of Pieter Brueghel the Elder and Bueckelaer, various paintings by Floris, portraits by V. Key and A. Mor, and works from the hands of the Mannerists. Numerous works by Rubens as well as paintings by van Dyck, Snyders, P. Vos, Honthorst, Pourbus, and David Tenier the Younger demonstrated values in Flemish painting. The Dutch were represented mostly by less important masters, but the Castle gallery did have one Rembrandt. It also had a Poussin, illustrating French classicism.

Works of art created at the Court of Rudolph II were included in the new collection—among them paintings by B. Spranger, H. von Aachen, J. Heintz, R. Savery, P. Stevens, G. Hoefnagel, and others. Great figures of the German Renaissance, such as Cranach, Dürer, Altdorfer, and Holbein, were equaled by those of the Baroque, such as A. Elsheimer, H. Schönfeld., C. Paudiss, S.Stosskopf, and J. von Sandrart. Spanish art included an outstanding portrait by Velásquez.

In the way it was arranged the new seventeenth-century collection, though still retaining many natural and artistic curios of Rudolph's day, was no longer a treasury in the old sense but a true gallery, aiming at variety in both subject and form. The walls of three elongated adjoining chambers, which formed a long corridor in the wing connecting the second and third Castle courtyards, were thickly hung with pictures in the same manner as Vienna's Stallburg, where Leopold Wilhelm's personal collection had found its home.

It should be stressed that the new Prague Castle Picture Gallery was no mere temporary exhibition or dependency of the Vienna collections, but a self-contained, independent complex, continuing the tasks and traditions of the former Bohemian art treasury as it had cared for the renowned collection of Rudolph II in the days before the Swedish invasion. This new gallery was administered by a royal Bohemian office in Prague, and remained untouched by imperial politicking for a long time. In the early eighteenth century, however, with the rise of Viennese centralism, the relationship between Vienna and the Czech lands began to change. Only when the relative independence of the Czech lands was abolished within the multinational Austrian state, did the pictures at Prague Castle come to be regarded as the Emperor's personal property and subjected to arbitrary shifts in location. This occurred under Charles IV, and the years 1721 and 1723 saw the first transports of selected works to Vienna. They included the best paintings by Titian and Veronese and works by Correggio, Andrea del Sarto, Poussin, Rubens, Strozzi, and Reni. The paintings that were subsequently brought to Prague in compensation did not equal them in quality. Among the most valuable pieces in the newly established gallery we have today are several pictures that escaped transfer and remained in Prague.

Further interference with the Prague Castle Picture Gallery was primarily the work of Empress Maria Theresa, who realized that ready money could be obtained by the sale of paintings at Prague Castle. She did not hesitate to offer an interested buyer—an agent who conducted secret negotiations on behalf of the Saxon Court—not only the 69 pieces he desired but the whole gallery, consisting at the time of 540 works. When eventually, in 1749, only 69 pictures found their way to Dresden to complete a deal made as early as 1742, this was not to Vienna's credit but was a consequence of the circumspect behavior of the Saxon Court and its well-considered and independent purchasing policy.

As already noted, the complex history of the gallery in the eighteenth century gave rise to a view that took root in the nineteenth century and that has stubbornly persisted until quite recently. It was that Prague lost its old famous collections as early as 1782 when the Castle became the scene of the notorious auction ordered by Joseph II. The story is more complicated than that. During the Prussian siege of Prague in 1757, the extensive collection at Prague Castle became disorganized. Some pictures, which had originally been kept in rooms set aside for that purpose for the duration of the siege, were moved to various places and subsequently wound up in Vienna. In the main, however, the collection was divided in two. One part was used to decorate chambers in the newly built Theresian Wing, and here the information about the origin of the individual paintings was soon lost; also, the old, valuable paintings were supplemented with numerous artistically second-rate paintings brought to Prague from Vienna for decorative purposes. The other part of the one-time gallery remained in the treasury and in other rooms of the Castle until the 1782 auction. At that time, everything that remained, including remnants of Rudolph II's collections, was presumably sold for next to nothing. It was this auction that gave rise to the belief that the entire Prague Castle Picture Gallery collection was sold. Forgotten was the fact that many of the old pictures were actually to be found among the paintings that decorated the chambers of the Theresian Wing.

The belief that Prague's treasures were gone was reinforced by further wholesale removals during the nineteenth century. In 1876, for example, Vienna had Alfred Woltmann reexamine the Prague Castle paintings. Many valuable pieces were identified, and practically anything that was regarded as worthy of notice was immediately transported to Vienna. In this way, 312 pictures in all reached Vienna in the years between 1865 and 1894. Nevertheless, a number of works did escape Woltmann's attention, the reason being that they were in a warehouse and thus regarded as material that had already been examined and consequently deserved no further notice.

Such was the condition of the collection and the prevailing views about it when Prague Castle was taken over by the newly established Republic in 1918. At that time, only a few paintings were examined by specialists, and they were turned over to the Gallery of the Society of Patriotic Friends of the Arts, which, with the Modern Gallery, was to become the foundation of the present-day National Gallery. The rest of the pictures remained merely as decoration in the individual rooms of the Castle or were stored away as unknown, unpublicized, and unexhibited works, regarded merely as historical documents of a bygone era. It was only in the 1960's that a professional reexamination restored the names of their creators to these forgotten masterpieces and gave them a new lease on life.

Among the preserved works, the paintings by the sixteenth-century Venetian masters, Titian, Tintoretto, Veronese, and Jacopo Bassano and his sons, form the most significant group. One work deserving the greatest measure of attention is Titian's *Portrait of a Young Woman at Her Toilet* (about 1520), regarded as an independent variant of his famous work in the Louvre. The original appearance of this work, which was cut to a smaller size in the eighteenth century, is borne out by an old copy in a private collection in England. In addition to its high quality, the authentic character of the work is established by numerous alterations that the artist made while working on the picture. These alterations, which were examined by X-ray, provide evidence of the painting's inner relationship to the Paris variant and prove that the creator must have been one and the same master.

Of great historical significance is the picture by Pordenone entitled *The Raising of Lazarus*, which had been regarded as missing for a long time. The painting had once belonged to the collection owned by Leopold Wilhelm and had been purchased by Basilius Fielding, British Ambassador, from the Marina family in Venice; it was described by Richardson in 1722 and again by Lessing in 1766. *The Flagellation of Christ* by Jacopo Tintoretto, a work conceived in a visionary manner, has great artistic value and is unique in the Czechoslovak collections; it was bought from the Buckingham Collection in 1648.

Particularly convincing specimens of the art of Paolo Veronese are the lyrically intense *St. Catherine and the Angel* and the insistently impressive *Portrait of Goldsmith Jakop Kinig (König)*. The epically conceived *Christ Washing the Feet of His Disciples* and 65

The Adoration of the Shepherds by the same master are part of a cycle of ten works on themes from the Old and New Testaments that had been purchased from the Buckingham Collection. Today seven works of this Veronese cycle are in Vienna, one in the National Gallery in Washington, while the remaining two are in Prague.

The art of Jacopo Bassano is represented by the sketchy *The Good Samaritan.* Jacopo's son, Francesco, painted the large *Christ's Presentation in the Temple* (once part of the Buckingham Collection) and *The Building of the Temple*, a freshly conceived and executed painting, which came to Prague from Leopold Wilhelm's Vienna collection. Thanks to their rich colors and communicativeness, the paintings by Leandro Bassano called *September* and *October*, the last pieces in Prague of a great cycle of the months, also are highly captivating (the other pieces in the cycle were moved to Vienna at the end of the nineteenth century). At one time Leopold Wilhelm's collection also contained the dramatic composition *Death of Niobe's Children*, which originated in the circle around Jacopo Tintoretto—probably from the hand of Antonio Vasilacchi.

Among works by Baroque masters, one of the most captivating is the gigantic painting by the young Rubens, *The Council of the Gods*, dating from the great Flemish master's early Italian period (about 1602), which serves to throw light on his artistic sources and development. Italian Baroque painting is worthily represented by Carlo Saraceni with a brilliantly executed *St. Sebastian* and, above all, by Domenico Fetti with his paintings *St. Jerome*, *Christ on the Mount of Olives*, and *The Sower of Tares*. The last of the three is part of the famous cycle which came to Prague some time in the 1650's from the Buckingham Collection and which was, with the exception of this one picture, sold to Dresden in 1742. As early as the seventeenth century, the painting by Guido Reni, *The Centaur Nessus and Deianeira*, was arousing admiration at Prague Cas-

tle, being preferred by the contemporary Swedish art expert and architect, Nicodemus Tessin, to the similar composition in Paris (today in the Louvre). The variety of Baroque painting in Italy is testified to at Prague Castle by works of Gentileschi, Massari, Stanzione, Keil, G. A. de Ferrari (?), Furini, and, above all, Codazzi.

Saturated with Neapolitan stimuli is the outstanding painting *The Battle of Joshua* by the German artist J. H. Schönfeld, while still in his Italian period. In the none too numerous collection of central European Baroque paintings that did not find their way to Prague until more recent times, the portraits of Jan Kupecký and the picturesque, robust paintings of Petr Brandl are endowed with a fascinating appeal. In addition to Dutch Mannerists, among whom Frederick van Valckenborch deserves special mention, the gallery has a group of Rudolphine masterpieces that recall the beginnings of the Prague Castle collections and, at the same time, are reminders of a chapter in the history of European art closely associated with Prague. They include pictures by Bartholomeus Spranger and Hans von Aachen as well as a number of outstanding designs by Adriaen de Vries, Rudolph's Court sculptor.

The current collection of about eighty works in the Prague Castle Gallery constitutes remnants from the former larger gallery. It is not a balanced, organic whole similar to the well-preserved ancient galleries, or modern ones, that have been built up methodically over time elsewhere in the world. Nevertheless, the gallery does have enough eminent works of art to permit it to group the exhibits into a collection capable of affording the viewer a captivating artistic experience. As a collection that is documentary in character, the gallery forms an historical pendant on the monumental architecture of Prague Castle and provides clear evidence of the impressively high level of its former artistic *ambiance*.

DESCRIPTION OF ILLUSTRATIONS

136 *St. Catherine and the Angel (Detail).* Paolo Caliari (called Veronese). Born 1528 in Verona, died 1588 in Venice. Canvas. Height 12 cm, width 54 cm. About 1580. Entered in inventory of Castle Gallery 1685, but probably in castle as early as 1655 to 56. Inv. No. O 26

137 *Christ Washing the Feet of His Disciples.* Paolo Caliari (called Veronese). Born 1528 in Verona, died 1588 in Venice. Canvas. Height 139 cm, width 283 cm. 1580's (toward close of artist's life). Part of painting, on left-hand side on surface of 34 × 37 cm, is Baroque addition. Painting, one part of cycle

of ten paintings whose subjects are taken from Old and New Testaments, was bought from Buckingham Collection in Antwerp 1648 or 1649. Entered in inventory of Castle Gallery 1685. Inv. No. D 218

138 *The Flagellation of Christ.* Jacopo Robusti (called Tintoretto). Born 1518 in Venice, died 1594 in Venice. Canvas. Height 165 cm, width 128.5 cm. About 1555. Composition of painting, square originally and cut in 18th century, could have been more or less imitated from similar composition of same period. Purchased in Antwerp 1648-49 from Buckingham Collection. Entered in inventory of Castle Gallery 1685. Inv. No. O 43

139 *The Good Samaritan.* Jacopo da Ponte (called Bassano). Born about 1515 at Bassano, died 1592 at Bassano. Canvas. Height 107 cm, width 84.5 cm. After 1550. Entered in inventory of Castle Gallery 1685. In castle probably as early as 1655-56. Inv. No. O 129

140 *The Sower of Tares.* Domenico Fetti. Born 1588 or 1589 in Rome, died 1623 in Venice. Oil on wood. Height 60.8 cm, width 44.5 cm. About 1621. Belongs to *Cycle of Parables.* Acquired from Buckingham Collection in Antwerp 1648-49 (formerly probably in Mantua). Entered in inventory of Castle Gallery 1685. Inv. No. O 25

141 *Allegory on Triumph of Loyalty over Fate.* Bartholomeus Spranger. Born 1546 in Antwerp, died 1611 in Prague. Allegory on fate of Jan Mont, sculptor and friend of Spranger's. Oil on wood. Height 52.5 cm, width 43.5 cm. 1607. On pedestal left below is following inscription: *INIQUA FATA (ITA) DECVS HOC | ORBI ET BELGIO | EREPTVM ITIS? | FIDES AEQUA | QVAE ETIAM | NOCTE SVA | (I) AM INVOLVTVM | PATRIAE ET LVCI | RESTI- TVIS.* On frame of pedestal below: *(A)DPICTUM ARCHETYPO IOH DE MONT GANDAVENSIS INTER PRIMOS AEVI HVIVS ET AVGVSTI CAES (ARIS) TATVARIOS DESCRIPSIT B. SPRAN- GERS DCVII.* Entered in inventory of Castle Gallery 1685, but had probably been in castle prior to that date. Inv. No. O 259

142 *Head of a Young Girl.* Hans von Aachen. Born 1552 in Cologne, died 1615 in Prague. Canvas. Height 51.3 cm, width 38 cm.

After 1610. Painting comes from Prague. First mentioned in inventory of Castle Gallery 1685. Inv. No. O 138

143 *The Centaur Nessus and Deianeira.* Guido Reni. Born 1575 in Bologna, died 1642 in Bologna. Canvas. Height 257 cm, width 195 cm. Before 1630. Later variant of composition in more mature style, which depicts following stage of action, is in Louvre. Entered in inventory of Castle Gallery 1685, but probably in castle as early as 1655-56. Inv. No. O 104

144 *The Council of the Gods.* Peter Paul Rubens. Born 1577 at Siegen in Westphalia, died 1640 in Antwerp. Canvas. Height 204 cm, width 374 cm. Probably 1602. Undoubtedly painted in Mantua, and under disguise of mythical scene is more a universal allegory aimed in concrete way at circles of Court in Mantua. Letter L with a colon right below is mark of unknown collection from which painting was purchased together with others. Entered in inventory of Castle Gallery 1685, probably in castle as early as 1655-56. Inv. No. O 102

145 *Portrait of Jan Oldřich Sichart.* Jan Kupecký. Born probably 1667 in Prague, died 1740 in Nürnberg. Canvas. Height 90.5 cm, width 70.5 cm. Between 1723 and 1726. Counterpart to portrait of Maria Magdalena Sichart. Identified from engraving by V. D. Preisler from year 1743. Acquired by Prague Castle 1934, prior to that property of Baron Geyso of Rottach. Inv. No. O 659

146 *Portrait of a Young Woman at Her Toilet.* Tiziano Vecellio (called Titian). Born probably between 1488 and 1490 at Pieve di Cadore, died 1576 in Venice. Canvas. Height 83 cm, width 79 cm. About 1520. Independent version of famous composition in Louvre. Old copy of work in private English collection and inventory list of 1737 prove that this painting originally was larger. Entered in inventory of Castle Gallery 1685, but certainly in castle as early as 1655-56. Inv. No O 34

147 *Paul the Apostle.* Petr Brandl. Born 1688 in Prague, died 1735 in Kutná Hora. Canvas. Height 91.5 cm, width 74.2 cm. After 1725. Below right signed in fragmentary way: (Petr)us Brandl Pinxit. Purchased from private collection 1933. In 1810 painting, which belonged to Count Josef Sweerts, was lent to Gallery of Society of Patriotic Friends of the Arts in Prague. Inv. No. O 557

STATE JEWISH MUSEUM

The collections of the State Jewish Museum in Prague are divided into three major exhibitions. The first presents the history and development of Jews in the Czech lands in documentary fashion. The other two are art collections that make accessible to the public two special sets of handicrafted objects: a collection of synagogue textiles and a collection of liturgical objects made of silver and other metals and used both in the synagogue and in the home. The start of these collections goes back to 1906, when the Prague Jewish religious community began gathering liturgical and secular objects from the former Prague Jewish Quarter. Gradually this led to a small Jewish Museum, which opened in 1909.

Of course, the vast part of the collections in what is today the State Jewish Museum came as a direct result of Nazi genocide during World War II, when the property of Bohemian and Moravian Jewish congregations—forcibly abolished by the Nazis—was concentrated in Prague. Thus, the collections bear witness to the barbarism of Nazism and memorialize the 100,000 Jewish citizens in the Czech lands who fell victim to the Nürnberg laws.

These collections, then, are valuable both historically and artistically. In order to preserve them, the State Jewish Museum was founded in 1950.

The collection of synagogue textiles in the Spanish synagogue comprises about eleven thousand items, which, in their entirety, exemplify the overall development of textile art in the Renaissance and Baroque periods in Bohemia and throughout Europe. Some of the curtains are exhibited in the synagogue, the rest are in depositories. In the Czech lands, *paroches* (curtains) and mantles (covers) for the Torah were made of imported French, Italian, and Spanish patterned silk combined with domestic embroidery. The donors rarely tried to be frugal about what it cost to produce these objects, which have great artistic value. Since the exhibits are well preserved, the patterns and technological processing of these ceremonial fabrics, with their designs in specific styles and with their examples of the domestic art of embroidery, constitute an instructive and complete survey of manufacturing methods in southern and western Europe.

Among the oldest exhibits is the material in the curtain at the Old-New Synagogue, which was donated by S. Jontoff. The Old-New Synagogue serves as a museum every day of the week except Saturday, when it is closed to the public to permit religious service to be held. Although the inscription applied in the upper part of the curtain dates it as late as 1638, the velvet brocade fabric, with its symetrically designed pomegranate pattern is of a substantially earlier date, pointing to Florence at the close of the fifteenth century as its place of origin. Likewise, other ancient curtains from Prague synagogues, donated by Mordechai Maisel and Jakob Baševi respectively, are made of precious Italian brocade. However, their finer flower design, arranged with strict symmetry and greater realism in elaboration, marks the origin of these ceremonial fabrics in the late sixteenth century. Another noteworthy specimen is the curtain of Noach Meir of Mladá Boleslav. It was not donated to the synagogue until 1744, but uses a Late Renaissance Italian brocade, dating from the close of the sixteenth century, whose pattern is one of horizontal friezes, containing the flower-vase motif. There is also quite a number of seventeenth-century Italian velvet brocades with strip and leaf decoration and crown motif.

Another interesting group is composed of curtains made of Spanish silk brocade with a Baroque design of large, impressively composed flowers and leaves. These come from synagogues at Lipník, Písek, and Rokycany as well as from Prague synagogues. French brocades, imported mainly from Lyons, began to appear in the eighteenth century. The older creations, made in the seventeenth century, have splendid decorative scroll motifs, followed in the eighteenth century by the gay, naturalist flower designs of the French Rococo and Classicism, arranged for the most part in vertical fashion along the wavy bands. Empire damasks and new, stylized geometric Turkish brocades complete the artistically valuable collection of ceremonial fabrics from Bohemian and Moravian synagogues in the State Jewish Museum.

Framing the fabric collection, in a sense, is the rich domestic embroidery, of which a substantial portion is formed in Hebrew dedicatory inscriptions, embroidered in gold thread. The inscriptions, usually in the upper part of the curtains and mantles, are in the shape of tablets inserted into the warp of the textile bordure. The latter is formed by differently decorated material or, in rare cases, is embroidered in the form of monopterons. Classical examples of such an architectonically composed curtain are the Maisel curtain made with appliqués, dating from 1593, and the curtain donated by J. Baševi in 1632; in the latter, the columns are covered by stylized carnations finely embroidered in gold. A particularly striking example of this type is the curtain donated by Löw Rosenberg to the Pinkas Synagogue in 1706 in which the lateral columns are coiled in form and surrounded by sculptural flowers. A late example, corresponding to the portal type of Early Baroque Christian altar, is the Nový Bydžov curtain dating from 1743. This architectonic solution is associated with synagogue curtains throughout the seventeenth and eighteenth centuries.

In many instances the inscriptions do not match the style of the hangings because old inscriptions were transferred to newer fabrics, and vice versa. Thus, for the most part, the synagogue curtains and mantles in the State Jewish Museum, with their precious textiles sewn together in differing designs, resemble tapestries like those created earlier in medieval European liturgic history, however, figure designs such as those encountered on draperies in

Gothic cathedrals were excluded. Rich decorative tasseling or band bordures further increase the value of the hangings.

In addition to the synagogue curtains and mantles, the Maisel Synagogue houses a permanent exhibition of precious synagogue objects in silver and gold. This display of over five hundred representative items is drawn from a collection of several thousand. Because of the nature of the exhibits and their value, both as cultural history and as artifacts, this collection, after those at Holy Cross Chapel in Prague Castle and the Loreto sanctuary, ranks as the third public exhibition in Prague most likely to attract visitors from at home and abroad.

Remarkable, too, is the craftsmanship, which gave artistic value to the work through the use of various techniques in shaping the precious metals. Indeed, the collection is both object lesson and historic documentation of the artistry that developed in Europe in the working of fine metals in the last five centuries. It also documents the high cultural and artistic level and technical craftsmanship of the domestic Bohemian, Moravian, and Silesian goldsmiths and silversmiths, whose works were drawn on so extensively by the Jewish congregations.

The collection does not include only items used for expressly religious purposes, such as Torah crowns, headpieces, Torah plate, and pointers, mezuzahs, menorahs, sets of Levite sacred utensils, alms boxes, bowls for citrus fruit, and spice containers; it also has objects of general use, such as pewterware, cups, and beakers. These traditional objects, too, were fashioned with the highest degree of style and art, and their creators are outstanding representatives of the goldsmith's and silversmith's craft, both native and foreign.

The State Jewish Museum collection has assembled a number of truly original specimens by identified masters in numerous goldsmith workshops. It is instructive to note certain economic aspects, such as the import of products made in Augsburg and Nürnberg; the ancient workshops in these communities were dominant at the close of the sixteenth century and in the seventeenth century, but, in the eighteenth and early nineteenth centuries, they yielded the palm to domestic production in Prague and Brno, which in turn had to give way to the competition of Vienna workshops during the period of the Empire and the Second Rococo. All these stages are illustrated in the State Jewish Museum collection, which contains some precious unique exhibits found only in Czechoslovakia. Goblets, pewterware, and citrus fruit holders stemming from the Augsburg workshops of the sixteenth, seventeenth, and early eighteenth centuries are especially rare in Europe. However, the appeal of these exhibits is exceeded by that of domestic work, which more than holds its own in artistic and technical design and execution in competition with products manufactured in other countries.

Two Brno pewter pieces, regrettably anonymous, originated in the first third of the seventeenth century, and the later gilded Banská Štiavnica goblet, which has the characteristic naturalistic ornamentation, belong to the period of European Mannerism. The Baroque period is represented by an exceptionally noble Levite set, with its outstanding arabesque pattern, dating from 1702, the work of the Prague goldsmith of the Lesser Quarter named Lux; by Prague and Brno seventeenth-century cups and bowls for citrus fruit, which by their strikingly hammered plant and fruit ornamentation echo foreign forms of production; and by High Baroque Torah plates from early eighteenth century.

The State Jewish Museum collection testifies to the fine artistic efforts of innumerable generations of craftsmen in Czechoslovakia and the whole of Europe. It is also an expression of the social, economic, and cultural relationships and conditions that prevailed through the centuries. Above all, the collection is a concentration of beautiful art objects, an expression of feeling and manual skill of past generations, and a constant inspiration to those who appreciate pure works of art and the conditions under which they originated.

DESCRIPTION OF ILLUSTRATIONS

148 *Synagogue Curtain.* Turnov. 1744. (Silk from France about 1750). Velvet, tinsel-embroidered, patterned silk material. Height 141 cm, width 200 cm. Inv. No. 57 264

149 *Jug of Burial Brotherhood.* Brno. Dated 1720 and 1801 (second making of jug). Pottery, painted burial scenes. Height 36.9 cm, diameter 16.5 cm. Inv. No. 8 049

150 *Torah Decoration* (Plate). Jan Jiří Kogler. Prague (Lesser Quarter). 1708. Gilded silver, chased, hammered and engraved. Height 45 cm, width 32.5 cm. Inv. No. 44 437

151 *Spice Container.* Brno. Mid-19th century. Silver, cast and engraved, unmarked. Height 8 cm, weight 30 g. Inv. No. 3988

152 *Spice Container.* G. Burda. Austria. 1807-1813. Silver, cast, chased, and engraved. Height 12.5 cm, weight 100 g. Originally from property of Old Jewish Museum (1909-1938). Inv. No. 12 744

153 *Spice Container.* Prague. End of 18th century. Silver, filigree, unmarked. Height 30.8 cm, weight 347 g. Inv. No. 173 855

154 *Torah Pennon* (Wedding Scene, detail). 1750. Pearl needlepoint lace on silk. Height 19.5 cm, width 200 cm. From the former Jewish congregation of Loštice in Moravia. Inv. No. 10 130

155 *Levite Set, Basin and Jug.* Jan Jiří Lux (1695-1724). Prague (Lesser Quarter). 1702. Silver, chased, wrought, engraved. Basin: Diameter 46.5 cm, weight 1,300 g. Jug: Height 22.5 cm, weight 480 g. Origin: Pinkas Synagogue, Prague. Inv. No. 46 036 a b

156 *Book; Seder zemirot u-birkat ha mazon* (Book of Benedictions). Published by Gershom Shelomo Kohen. Prague, October 30, 1514 (date of end of printing). Print decked with woodcuts, some of them hand-colored. Book: Height 16.7 cm, width 13.7 cm. Illustrations: Height 6 cm, width 9.7 cm. Inv. No. 168 451

157 *Pewter Set.* Bohemia. Mid-18th century. Engraved decoration. Plate: Diameter 30 cm. Jug: Height 24.5 cm. Acquired 1964. Inv. No. 173 118

158 *Book; Haggada shel pesah (Passover Service).* Published by Gershom Shelomo Kohen. Prague, December 30, 1526 (date of end of printing). Print decked with woodcuts. No Inv. No.

The history of Czechoslovak military museums is, to an extraordinary degree, closely linked to the historical destinies of the people of Czechoslovakia. At the time the Czech lands and Slovakia formed part of Austria-Hungary, conditions were hardly favorable for the establishment of an institution that would concern itself with documenting the country's military past. Only the founding of the independent Czechoslovak state in 1918 made such an institution possible and, what is more, desirable and necessary.

At the outset, attention was mainly focused on the struggle, both political and military, waged by members of the Czech and Slovak nations against Austria-Hungary during the first world war. However, the Liberation Memorial, established in 1919–1920, was conceived as a complex institution whose aim was to go beyond documenting Czech and Slovak resistance of that period. Of course the history of the resistance and its problems were to be studied and written records of political resistance organizations and of the Czechoslovak Legions (the fighting military units) abroad preserved. But equally important, materials recalling these struggles were to be collected and organized for exhibition by the museum section.

The military history of Czechoslovakia did not begin with the resistance against the Hapsburg monarchy, however. For centuries, an independent Czech state had maintained its own armed forces for use in the struggle to be independent. Even in the period when the Czech state became part of the Austro-Hungarian monarchy and its own armed forces gradually ceased to exist, the break in the country's military and war history was not complete. This, no doubt, was one of the reasons that led the Ministry of National Defense in 1920 to entrust the then Czechoslovak Institute of Military Science with the task of "building up a Czechoslovak war museum in Prague in order to safeguard all the historical monuments which are of significance in the history of warfare." This was the idea behind the creation of the second Czechoslovak military museum. Under the name of Military Museum of the Czechoslovak Republic, it undertook, in the years between the two world wars, to collect and assemble materials on fighting and warfare, with particular reference to the territory of Czechoslovakia.

Thus the Czechoslovak military museums developed along two substantially different lines and in two separate institutions. Starting in 1926, the Museum of the Liberation Memorial was situated in a section of the Memorial's new building equipped especially for it in accordance with plans drawn by the building's architect, J. Zázvorka. Not long after, the collections of the Military Museum of the Czechoslovak Republic were opened to the public and subsequently moved to the Baroque buildings of the Prague *Invalidovna* (Military Home for Disabled Soldiers). From the beginning, the latter museum focused primarily on systematically collecting objects of a military character. It also established a large library of books on "militaria" derived from the Thun Library. Changes resulting from the reorganization of the hitherto existing Institute of Military Science by the end of the 1920's did not produce any modification in the dual purposes and programs of the Czechoslovak military museums. Although the Military Museum of the Czechoslovak Republic was technically subordinated to the Liberation Memorial, both museums remained autonomous until 1939.

Nazi occupation of the Czech lands had disastrous consequences for both Czechoslovak military museums and their activities. The military occupation authorities were not slow to liquidate both museums and set up what was called the *Heeresmuseum Prag*, which was housed in the Renaissance building of the former Švarcenberk Palace. The occupation authorities went all out to gather together in the *Heeresmuseum* the most significant collections of weapons and arms from the Czech lands, taking over among others the collection of the d'Este family in the Konopiště Castle and confiscating the Lobkowicz collections at Roudnice and a number of others. However, the long prepared opening of the *Heeresmuseum* did not materialize, nor did these collections wind up in Hitler's notorious "supermuseum," which was in the process of being formed in Linz. Realizing that defeat was inevitable, the occupation authorities had the most important items of the collections moved to places outside of Czechoslovakia.

The liberation of Czechoslovakia by the Soviet Army at the end of World War II in May, 1945, made it possible to revive the Czechoslovak military museums. The Military Museum of the Czechoslovak Republic of preoccupation days resumed its activities under the name of Military Historical Museum. In the early years after liberation, it was largely responsible for having the military, artistic, and historical collections that had been taken out of Czechoslovakia brought back home.

The social changes that occurred in Czechoslovakia were clearly reflected in all the Military Historical Museum's activities, and particularly in the substantial enlargement of its collections. These were greatly enriched by property confiscated from traitors and collaborationists and by collections that the state acquired as a result of nationalization. Material objects that documented military activities, particularly on the soil of Czechoslovakia, were collected, and attention was paid to the development of the fighting traditions of the Czechoslovak people. Care was also taken to trace the development of the making of arms in Bohemia. Although the beginnings of this orientation can be traced back to the period between the two wars, real progress in the business of collecting was due primarily to the changes that came with the building of socialism in Czechoslovakia. For instance, the collections of artillery pieces assembled by the Škoda Works in Plzeň became the property of the Military Historical Museum, which gradually also became the administrator of a substantial part of the technical collections of *Zbrojovka*, the armament works of Brno.

Following liberation in 1945, the Museum of the Liberation Memorial also widened its scope considerably, primarily to include material documenting the struggle of the Czech and Slovak people against fascism and the occupation, both inside the country itself and on the military fronts abroad. Subsequently, it included documentary material on the development of the Czechoslovak Army in general. In the 1950's this new aspect of the museum's collecting, scientific, and educational activities was acknowledged in the institution's new name, Czechoslovak Army Museum.

For a number of years the parallel existence of the two military museums, each a part of the Institute of Military History, went on unimpaired, although changes in the direction of their respective activities did result in an ever closer rapprochement between them. In 1962, these changes culminated in their merger into a single institution, the Military Museum in Prague.

The focus of the Czechoslovak military museums is clearly reflected in the contents and character of the collections now assembled in the Military Museum in Prague. Thus, the overwhelming majority of the exhibits represents a record of the military activities of particular men, most of whom are related to the military history of the territory of Czechoslovakia. However, some sets have acquired the broader character of systematically assembled collections. This is particularly true of the extensive collection of small firearms (about six thousand items). This collection affords an almost complete survey of developments in this kind of weapon the world over and is especially rich in items dating from the advent of breech loading and the repeating rifle in the second half of the nineteenth century. Efforts to assemble documentation on the production of firearms within the country itself from their origin in the fourteenth and fifteenth centuries to the beginning of the nineteenth century are also best reflected in this small-arms collection. Bohemian masters from the seventeenth to the early nineteenth century are represented by several hundred pieces, which are interesting primarily from the technical point of view. At the

74

same time, many of them are clear evidence of the high standard achieved in this craft in Bohemia.

Among the most significant collections are objects by a number of Czech designers (Sylvestr and Karel Trnka, among others), acquired through bequests. Particularly noteworthy are the numerous collections of specimens demonstrating technical development which have been assembled in Czechoslovak armaments works (at Brno and at Strakonice).

The core of the collection of old weapons and armor is the systematic assemblage of weapons and arms employed by the Hapsburg armies and the numerous exhibits relating to other European countries, particularly those whose armed forces engaged in fighting on the territory of present-day Czechoslovakia. Of the older weapons, those worthy of special mention are a number of fine medieval swords and a relatively large collection of arms and armor dating from the Renaissance and Baroque periods. Some of the items in this last group, mainly those from central and southern Europe, are on a high artistic level.

In addition to medieval pieces, the collections of artillery have numerous specimens from the sixteenth to eighteenth century. The culminating achievement is the already mentioned collection of the Plzeň Škoda Works, which contains unique specimens of historical value, showing the first attempts, at the turn of the twentieth century, to create modern quick-firing artillery.

A new section, only recently made accessible to the public, is the aviation collection. Close to one hundred models of aircraft supplement the large number of air force arms and aircraft engines on display.

In the collection of military uniforms, exhibits dating from the nineteenth and twentieth centuries predominate. Perhaps special mention should be made of the uniform once worn by Marshal Alfred von Windischgrätz, who acquired notoriety for suppressing the Prague uprising in the revolution of 1848, and the collection of uniforms once belonging to Ferdinand d'Este. Particularly valuable exhibits in the collection are those from the second world war, which are mostly uniforms presented to the museum by leading participants in the struggle against the Nazi occupation forces. Worthy of special note is a number of memorial items of Army General Ludvík Svoboda and parts of uniforms of Soviet marshals and generals who took part in the liberation of Czechoslovakia in the years 1944–1945.

One of the richest is the collection of Orders and Decorations, numbering about five thousand items. It includes extremely precious and unique specimens, most of which are connected with outstanding military figures in the Czech lands and Slovakia.

The oldest exhibits in the collection of flags and standards date back to the early eighteenth century. The most numerous are regimental colors of Austro-Hungarian regiments recruited on Czechoslovak territory. There is a complete collection of banners and standards of Czechoslovak Army regiments in the period between the world wars. Among the most valuable other standards are those under which Czechoslovak units fought against fascism on various fronts during World War II.

The museum also has extensive collections of an iconographic nature, the core of which is a group of drawings, dating from the sixteenth to eighteenth century. Exhibits of iconographic material from the nineteenth century are also fairly numerous. Among the more interesting exhibits is the collection of paintings by leading Czech and Slovak landscape artists, showing the battlements on which units of the Czechoslovak legions abroad fought. In keeping with the nature of a military museum, the decisive criterion in collecting objects of this kind is necessarily their iconographic significance; nevertheless, most of the paintings are also true works of art.

In addition to its own collections, the Military Museum is responsible for housing a number of deposits entrusted to its care by Czechoslovak authorities. The most important of these are collections of outstanding specimens of arms and armor from the castles of Konopiště and Roudnice.

At the present time, all the main exhibits in the Military Museum are being given scientific treatment, and a scientific catalogue of the most significant sections of the collections is gradually being prepared. There is one major task for the museum staff: research into the material and technical basis of military art and warfare in our own territory, with particular reference to the making of arms in the Middle Ages, in the period of the rise of a standing army, and in the period when the modern Czechoslovak armaments industry developed. 75

DESCRIPTION OF ILLUSTRATIONS

159 *Romanesque Sword.* Site of find unknown. Second half of 11th century. May have belonged to Siguin, Archbishop of Cologne (1079-1089). Preserved length 92 cm. Hilt lined with silver, brass, copper, and gold with themes from Old and New Testaments. Quillons lined with same precious metals in oblique bands. Blade bears engraved inscription *SIGVINAIS* originally inlaid with fine iron wire. Collection d'Este, Konopiště, Inv. No. 477 E; Military Museum, Prague. Inv. No. D 237

160 *Italian Dagger (Cinquedea).* Workshop of Ercole dei Fideli. Ferrara. 1480-1500. Length 65.5 cm. Hilt of horn with brass mounting; mounted on both sides with silver band bearing inscription: EXIGO PENAS—ERO PARCE. Quillons chased and gilded with ornamental band depicting trophies of arms. Central locket missing. In upper part of blade etched and gilded decoration. Below two ornamental belts and inscription FIDES is figure worked after antique pattern. On other side ornaments and figures without inscription. In central part engraved and gilded circle with female figures. Collection d'Este, Konopiště, Inv. No. 350 E; Military Museum, Prague, Inv. No. D 242

161 *Wheel-lock Rifle (Detail).* Georg A. Feiler. Karlovy Vary. End of 17th century. Total length 113.5 cm. Barrel marked G. Feiler A.C. Badt, decorated with engraved scrolled foliage and gold inlaid flowers. Cock carved with figures and trophies. Polished lock plate marked G.F. and decorated with carved motifs of war trophies. Butt of rare exotic wood with ebony and bone accessories. Collections of Dr. J. V. Hefner-Alteneck, auction catalogue 1904, No. 123. From Museum of Decorative Art, Prague. Transferred to Military Museum in 1962; Inv. No. II-1 572

162 *Wheel-lock Rifle (Detail).* Leopold Becher the Elder. Karlovy Vary. About 1726-1728. Total length 101 cm. Barrel browned and marked with gold incrustation *LEOPOLD BECHER B.* Lock richly cut with motif of Fortune and other figurative elements. Lock plate marked: L. Becher. Butt decorated with silver-wire incrustation, casing with rich relief iron engraving of rifle range of the day. Lobkowicz Collection, Roudnice Castle, Inv. No. XII/Cb-4; Military Museum, Prague, Inv. No. D 870

163 *Bronze Barrel.* Northern Italy, Toscana (?). Last quarter of 15th century. Length 158 cm. Cast brass barrel of four parts, which are screwed together in reinforced points. Mouth in shape of dragon's head; richly articulated filigree. Collection d'Este, Konopiště, Inv. No. 987 E; Military Museum, Prague, Inv. No. SM 5922

164 *Pair of Stirrups.* Unknown master. Prague. Second half of 16th century. Cut iron. Height 19.5 cm. Part of property of Ladislav II, Popel of Lobkowicz (?-1584), or of his son Zdeněk Vojtěch (1568-1628). All parts richly engraved in geometrical band and vegetable ornament with zoomorphic motifs. In sides of box for stirrup, leather coats of arms of Counts of Lobkowicz are cut. Crossed escutcheon, first and fourth field halved, in second and third fields eagle. Lobkowicz Collection, Roudnice, Inv. No. XIII/ k-9; Military Museum, Prague, Inv. No. D 1 817

165 *Helmet (Pear-shaped Morion).* Northern Italy. Third quarter of 16th century. Height 26 cm. Vertical division of bell in three fields chased and gilded with motifs of ornaments, trophies, and figures. Decoration close to Pisa style of school of Pompeo della Casa. Collection d'Este, Konopiště, Inv. No. 234 E; Military Museum, Prague, Inv. No. D 126

ILLUMINATED MANUSCRIPTS
IN PRAGUE LIBRARIES

Prague, capital of the country that was predestined to become the crossroads of various cultural influences by virtue of its geographic position in Europe, transformed them, in turn, to her own image. This is true in art as in politics, and nowhere more so than in the collections of manuscripts. In addition to the manuscripts that were the foundation stones of the country's literary culture, Prague also has a large number of illuminated codices that permit us to follow the development of literary art in Bohemia since the late eleventh century. Some of these works are of such artistic importance that they have had an impact on the illumination of books throughout the world.

Most of the illuminated codices are concentrated in three institutions, whose history can be traced over centuries. These are the Archives in Prague Castle (the former Chapter Library, *Knihovna Kapitulní*, in St. Vitus' Cathedral), the State Library of the Czech Socialist Republic (above all the stock of the old University Library), and the National Museum Library. In addition to these large collections, more manuscripts can be found, particularly in archives, for example, in the Central State Archives and in the Archives of the City of Prague, at Charles University, and in a number of small institutions.

Some of the monastery libraries are still kept at their original, ancient sites. The most important of these is the Strahov Library, which at present is part of the Memorial of National Literature, now housed in the monastery building. The importance of the Strahov Library, however, lies in its rare sets of printed literature rather than the antiquity of its collection. Since the monastery burned down on several occasions, the original library was not preserved and the present manuscript collection was not begun until the eighteenth century. In other Prague monastery libraries, the administration of which has now been entrusted to public institutions, libraries, and archives, outstanding illuminated manuscripts are the exception.

Large as the Prague collections are, they do not by any means exhaust the wealth of manuscripts in Czechoslovakia. Libraries outside of Prague and most of the regional institutes have extensive collections of their own as well as those originally assembled in castles and monasteries. Since the end of the second world war, these have been made accessible for study by Czechoslovak and foreign researchers. Some historical sets have remained in their original surroundings; others have been moved to one of the larger institutions, where they have been kept as independent collections. All the collections contain many illuminated manuscripts of foreign origin. Codices dating from earlier times are predominantly liturgical books, but for later periods, one can find examples of secular literature. There are also fine French books of hours preserved for the most part in the libraries of the aristocracy.

The most ancient collection in Prague is in the St. Vitus' Cathedral Chapter Library, administered by the Archives of Prague Castle (the chapter was closely associated with the metropolitan cathedral from the days of its founding). References to some manuscripts gradually acquired for St. Vitus' have been found in chronicles and other sources; starting in the middle of the fourteenth century, it is possible to trace the individual codices from inventories that have been preserved. The collection started primarily with liturgical books, later augmented by gifts from church dignitaries and manuscripts from monasteries that ceased to exist during the Hussite period.

Among the most ancient illuminated codices is the *Carolingian Gospel Book*, dating from the ninth century. It is richly ornamented with figures and has a good number of full-page illustrations representing single biblical persons, and initials at the beginning of each Gospel. The binding dates from the fourteenth century and is of gilded copper plate set with semiprecious stones; the front cover bears a small ivory plate from the fourth century with the figure of St. Peter.

The Bohemian codices include the *Gospel Book*, dating from the end of the eleventh century, which probably came from the same workshop as the *Coronation Gospel Book (Codex Vyšehradensis)*, which contains full-page pictures of the Evangelists. One codex, dating from the first half of the twelfth century (about 1136–1137), comes from the workshop of Hildebert and Evervin and depicts a vivid scene of scribes, while the *Codex Ostroviensis* and *De civitate Dei* of St. Augustine go back to about 1200. The development of illumination art in Bohemia during the reigns of Charles IV and Wenceslas IV, in the second half of the fourteenth century, can also be traced in the codices, particularly in those that Arnošt of Pardubice (Ernst von Pardubitz), Prague's first archbishop, in about 1360 commissioned for St. Vitus' Cathedral. Others were works ordered by Jan of Středa (Johannes von Neumarkt), Bishop of Litomyšl and later Olomouc and Charles' Chancellor.

It is hard to detect changes in the Bohemian art of illumination during the fifteenth century, as rich and simple illuminations alike continue to show the influences of the late fourteenth century. The St. Vitus collection of illuminated manuscripts ends in a number of graduals going back to the sixteenth century, among which the most remarkable is the Latin gradual of 1552 from the workshop of Jan Táborský and Fabián Puléř.

The development of the University Library, forming the oldest part of the State Library of the Czech Socialist Republic, starts with works from the mid-fourteenth century. In the rich collection of manuscripts, those dating from the earliest times are more often not illuminated, as they were required by the university for purposes of study. Yet even among the codices of a more instructional nature, some, including a number of books of foreign origin, are decorated with a few painted initials.

Some of these codices were acquired through bequests by burghers who chose to remember the domestic academic institutions more because of their public significance than their scientific importance during the Hussite period.

Most of the illuminated manuscripts in the University Library were not acquired until the end of the eighteenth century when some religious orders were abolished and their libraries transferred to the Clementinum in Prague. That was how the library acquired manuscripts from the most ancient of the convents in Czechoslovakia, the Benedictines of St. George at Prague Castle. Included among the manuscripts were the magnificent *Passional of Abbess Kunhuta* and a number of codices from south Bohemian monasteries in Třeboň, Český Krumlov, and Zlatá Koruna, the latter containing codices donated by the Lords of Rožmberk. It was during this period, too, that the Clementinum came into possession of the *Codex Vyšehradensis*, dating from the end of the eleventh century; the *Sedlec Antiphonary*, dating from the mid-thirteenth century; the Czech manuscript of the "Six Books" *(Knížky šestery)* by Thomas of Štítný (dating from 1376, it is a product of the supreme art of book making of the Luxemburg period); the beautiful *Breviary* of Beneš of Valdštejn, and a number of Czech bibles, the finest specimen of which is the *Bible* made in the fifteenth century and belonging later to the library of Sixt of Ottersdorf.

After the first world war, the University Library was enriched by a large collection of manuscripts from the Prague Lobkovicz Library, which originally contained such precious items as the illustrated *Velislav Bible*, dating from the middle of the fourteenth century, and the *Lobkovicz Breviary* of 1494, one of the earliest Renaissance illuminated manuscripts in the collection. After the second world war, the University Library was entrusted with the care of a substantial number of manuscripts that significantly enriched the older collections.

Noteworthy among the castle libraries is the Lobkovicz Library from Roudnice, which can be traced as far back as the fifteenth century. It included several fine manuscripts from the Luxemburg period, such as the *Rožmberk Orationale* containing prayers in the Czech vernacular instead of Latin. The most ancient codices from the collection of the Premonstratensian Monastery at Teplá are now assembled in Prague; they include a number of religious manuscripts dating from the thirteenth and fourteenth centuries—the *Prayers* of Ladislav Posthumus, written by Johannes of Ulm, and codices owned by Abbot Zikmund, restorer of the monastery toward the end of the fifteenth century. The most important illuminated manuscript in these collections is the *Breviary* of Leo, Grand Master of Knights of the Cross with a Red Star, written in 1356, one of the most precious specimens of the art of illumination of that period.

All these sets also include interesting illuminated manuscripts of foreign origin. Above all, there are French manuscripts in both Lobkovicz libraries. Older German illuminated manuscripts of the Prague Lobkovicz Library, like those coming from the Premonstratensian Monastery at Swabian Weissenau, are particularly striking.

The National Museum Library is the newest of the major historical libraries in Prague; it also developed somewhat differently from the Chapter Library and the University Library. Soon after its founding 160 years ago, the National Museum acquired the collection of the Březnice Castle Library, a donation from Count Kolovrat-Krakovský, and the collection of Václav Leopold Chlumčanský, Archbishop of Prague, which together formed the foundation of the museum's outstanding collection of illuminated manuscripts. Donations by the Czech towns of Plzeň, Tábor, and others helped the growth of the collection.

As with the two older libraries, the National Museum Library can trace, in its own collections, the development of the art of illumination in Bohemia. Among the earliest codices is the *Mater verborum*, dating from the first half of the thirteenth century—a point of special interest is the preservation of the Czech glosses on this codex. Another early codex is the *Latin Bible*, showing the Italian-Byzantine influence and written around 1300; it originated in the St. Francis Monastery in the New Town of Prague, and is apparently the only item extant from what once must have been the monastery's rich collections. Somewhat younger is the *Missal* (before the mid-fourteenth century), formerly the property of Jan of Dražice, Bishop of Prague; it contains an interesting canon leaf.

The National Museum's finest codices are from the second half of the fourteenth century and constitute an excellent source for studying the art of illumination in Bohemia in that period. In addition to the *Prayer Book* of Arnošt of Pardubice, two especially noteworthy codices can be compared with the finest in the world. The first of these is the *Liber viaticus* (Breviary) written for Jan of Středa (Johannes von Neumarkt), one of the most magnificent codices of Bohemian origin. The rich paintings in the margins depict vivid, realistic scenes, and the large initials and fine handwriting make up a unified array of pages marked with the bishop's name. The other prominent codex is the *Laus Mariae*, the work of Conradus de Haimburg, completed before 1364; both his full-page miniatures are in the same style as contemporary paintings. Among the great number of liturgical manuscripts from the period, special prominence should be given to the *Plzeň Missal* by Jan of Strniště, dating from the early fifteenth century. The *Cheb Officium of St. Jerome* was written in 1404 by Jan of Šitboř. In the introductory miniature, no lesser figure than the writer himself, Jan of Šitboř, who is also the author of the outstanding medieval poem *Der Ackermann aus Böhmen (The Ploughman of Bohemia)*, is on his knees before Saint Jerome.

The early fifteenth century (around 1420) is when the Czech collection of religious and mystic tracts, called the *Krumlovský sborník* (Krumlov Codex), originated at Český Krumlov. It contains a large number of miniatures with scenes from both the Old and New Testaments. The "fine Bohemian style" can subsequently be noted in a number of codices dating from the fifteenth century. In a rather different style are the ornamentation and illustrations of the outstanding Hussite item referred to as the *Codex of Jena*, in which are depicted antithetic scenes from the life of the original church and from that of the contemporary church, with all the evils committed by its practitioners. The codex is the work of several artists; some of the pictures are by the illuminator Janíček Zmilelý of Písek, with whose name one associates the Hussite scenes (some even portray Jan Žižka, leader of the Hussite army). This rare Hussite document had been in the University of Jena Library since the middle of the sixteenth century; it was returned to its place of origin as a gift of Wilhelm Pieck, President of the German Democratic Republic, in 1951.

The National Museum Library has been entrusted with the administration and care of a number of other libraries. One of these, which now bears the name of Josef Dobrovský (formerly the Nostitz Library), contains an interesting illuminated codex of Bohemian origin, dating from the end of the fourteenth century, the *Bible of Kuneš, the Altar Custodian*. Among other duties the National Museum Library is charged with the administration of castle libraries, many of which are still in their original sites. One of the most significant of these is the Kynžvart (formerly Metternich) Library, which possesses a great number of important manuscripts. These collections are gradually being sorted out, classified, and made accessible for study and, not infrequently, new discoveries.

As already mentioned, a number of individual codices can be found in other institutions. It is regrettable that no manuscripts have been preserved from the earliest days of the Strahov Monastery, which was founded as early as the twelfth century, but, as already noted, was destroyed and rebuilt several times. One of the earliest codices now preserved in the Strahov Library is the *Gospel Book* of the late tenth century, which originated in the St. Martin's Monastery in Treves; an interesting feature is its binding, which combines elements from the twelfth to the seventeenth century. Among the manuscripts classified as belonging to the "fine Bohemian style" are the *Pontifical Book* of Albert of Šternberk, dating from 1376 and the *Missal* of 1482 from the Louka Monastery.

Among the smaller sets, mention must be made of the outstanding *Gradual*, written by Friar Jacob, from the Dominican monastery at St. Giles (Jiljí) in the Old Town of Prague, which dates from the very beginning of the fifteenth century; this gradual used to be private property, and in 1948 it was presented to Charles University where it is deposited in the Institute for the Charles University's History.

In the collections of illuminated manuscripts in all institutions, it is interesting to note that we can trace not only the development of the art of painters and scribes but also the fact that from the fourteenth century patrons of this art form included secular persons, the aristocracy and burghers, and not just the holy orders. The contribution of secular persons in ordering codices is of particular significance in the sixteenth century, when, for the brotherhoods of lay burgher singers established at the individual churches, large graduals and other hymn books were produced, richly ornamented with paintings that frequently depicted scenes from contemporary urban life. These hymn books were originally also evidence of the esteem in which Magister John Hus was held even in divine liturgical songs. Scenes depicting the burning of John Hus were cut out of many of the codices, but by fortunate coincidence some of the other codices escaped this Counter Reformation censorship. At the time of the abolition of the literary brotherhoods toward the end of the eighteenth century, these codices were assembled in public institutions and nowadays are often the pride even of some of the smaller museums.

Although the present Czechoslovak collections of illuminated manuscripts are sufficiently well-rounded to permit one to study the development of the art of book making in Bohemia, it should be borne in mind that they are not really complete. During the past centuries several outstanding literary monuments were taken abroad in one way or another, and are still missing.

DESCRIPTION OF ILLUSTRATIONS

166 *Christ in Mandorla.* From *Codex Vyšehradensis*, Coronation Gospel Book. About 1085. Prepared presumably for coronation of Vratislav II. Richly illuminated parchment codex containing 24 full-page illustrations and many decorative illuminations. Height 42 cm, width 33 cm. State Library of Czech Socialist Republic XIV A 13, fol. 9v

167 *Heavenly Jerusalem.* St. Augustine. From *De civitate Dei.* About 1200. Parchment codex decorated with rich initials. Height 39.5 cm, width 28 cm. In the lower right-hand corner are four figures (bishop, monk, man, and woman) marked with the inscription *Boemenses*. Archives of Prague Castle, formerly Chapter Library (*Kapitulní knihovna*) of St. Vitus' Cathedral A 7, fol. 1v

168 *Madonna on Throne.* Psalter. From *Codex Ostroviensis.* About 1200. Parchment codex with three full-page illustrations and rich initials. Height 31 cm, width 20 cm. From Benedictine

Monastery at Ostrov near Davle. Archives of Prague Castle, formerly Chapter Library *(Kapitulní knihovna)* of St. Vitus' Cathedral A 57/I, fol. 10v

169 *The Three Marys and Angel at Christ's Open Tomb.* From *Sedlec Antiphonary.* First half of 13th century. Miniature with inserted initial A, parchment codex with 15 miniatures. Height 44.5 cm, width 32 cm. Originally written for one of Cistercian convents, later deposited in Cistercian monastery at Sedlec near Kutná Hora. State Library of Czech Socialist Republic XIII A 6, p. 173

170 *Building of Tower of Babylon.* From illustrated bible called *Velislav Bible.* About 1340. Richly illuminated parchment codex. Height 30.5 cm, width 24 cm. Written for Velislav the Prothonotary. From Monastery Library of Knights of the Cross with Red Star in Prague it was transferred to Lobkovicz Library in Prague. State Library of Czech Socialist Republic XXIII C 124, fol. 11v

171 *Annunciation of Our Virgin.* Conradus de Haimburg. From *Laus Mariae.* Before 1364. Parchment codex with two full-page miniatures. Height 30 cm, width 20 cm. National Museum Library XVI D 13, fol. 55v

172 *Stigmatization of St. Francis of Assisi.* From *Vitae* (Lives of the Fathers), in Czech translation by Řehoř Hrubý of Jelení. 1516. Parchment codex. Height 49 cm, width 36 cm. With numerous initials and depicting scenes from lives of saints, and with richly ornamented leaf margins. In lower left-hand corner is kneeling Chancellor Ladislav of Šternberk who ordered codex. State Library of Czech Socialist Republic XVII A 2, fol. 2v

173 *Christ's Mystic Embrace with Mary.* From *Passional of Abbess Kunhuta.* Prague. 1314-1321. Richly illuminated parchment codex. Height 30 cm, width 24.5 cm. Collection of mystic tracts by Dominican Friar Kolda of Koldice, written for Kunhuta, abbess at Benedictine Convent at St. George's in Prague Castle. State Library of Czech Socialist Republic XIV A 17, fol. 16v

174 *Annunciation of Our Virgin in initial G(audeamus).* From *Liber viaticus Joannis Noviforensis.* 1360-1364. Parchment codex with many illuminations. Height 43.5 cm, width 31 cm. Written for Jan of Středa (Johannes von Neumarkt), the Bishop of Olomouc, formerly of Litomyšl, and Charles IV's Chancellor. From the collection of V. L. Chlumčanský, Archbishop of Prague. National Museum Library XII A 12, fol. 69v

175 *St. Jerome at Writing Stand.* From *Officium of St. Jerome.* Cheb. 1404. Parchment codex containing richly decorated title page. Kneeling before St. Jerome is writer of codex Jan of Šitboř (from Žatec), author of composition *Der Ackermann von Böhmen* (The Ploughman of Bohemia). National Museum Library XIII A 18, fol. 1r

176 *Initial S with Kneeling King David.* From *Lobkovicz Breviary.* 1494. Parchment codex with full-page illustrations, preceded by Lobkovicz coat of arms. Height 17.5 cm, width 12 cm. Illuminator was probably Matouš of Kutná Hora. Hunting scene in rich ornamental framework. State Library of Czech Socialist Republic XXIII F 202, fol. 88r

177 *Hussite Mass.* From *Codex of Jena, Antithesis Christi et Antichristi.* Prague. About 1500. Richly illuminated parchment and paper codex containing 88 full-page illustrations some of which were painted by Janíček Zmilelý of Písek. Height 31.5 cm, width 21.5 cm. Gift of President of German Democratic Republic Wilhelm Pieck to Czechoslovakia in 1951. National Museum Library IV B 24, fol. 55v

178 *John the Evangelist.* From *Gospel-Book of St. Martin's Monastery in Treves.* End of 10th century. Parchment codex. Memorial of National Literature, Strahov Library D F III 3

179 *Binding.* From *Gospel Book of St. Martin's Monastery in Treves.* 12th to 17th century. Red velvet with enamel disks, gilded figures, medallions, and semiprecious stones. Height 29.5 cm, width 18 cm. Part of silver corners on back plate and two buckles are preserved. Memorial of National Literature, Strahov Library D F III 3

PICTURE CREDITS

NATIONAL MUSEUM

Bronze Hatchet with Disk-like Back and Pair of Cuff-like Bracelets. Second half of 2nd millennium B.C.

2 *Argillite Sculpture of Head of Celtic Deity*. End of 2nd century B.C.

Gold Chain with Medallion and Small Silver Plate with Relief of Stag, from Slavonic Barrow. 9th century A.D.

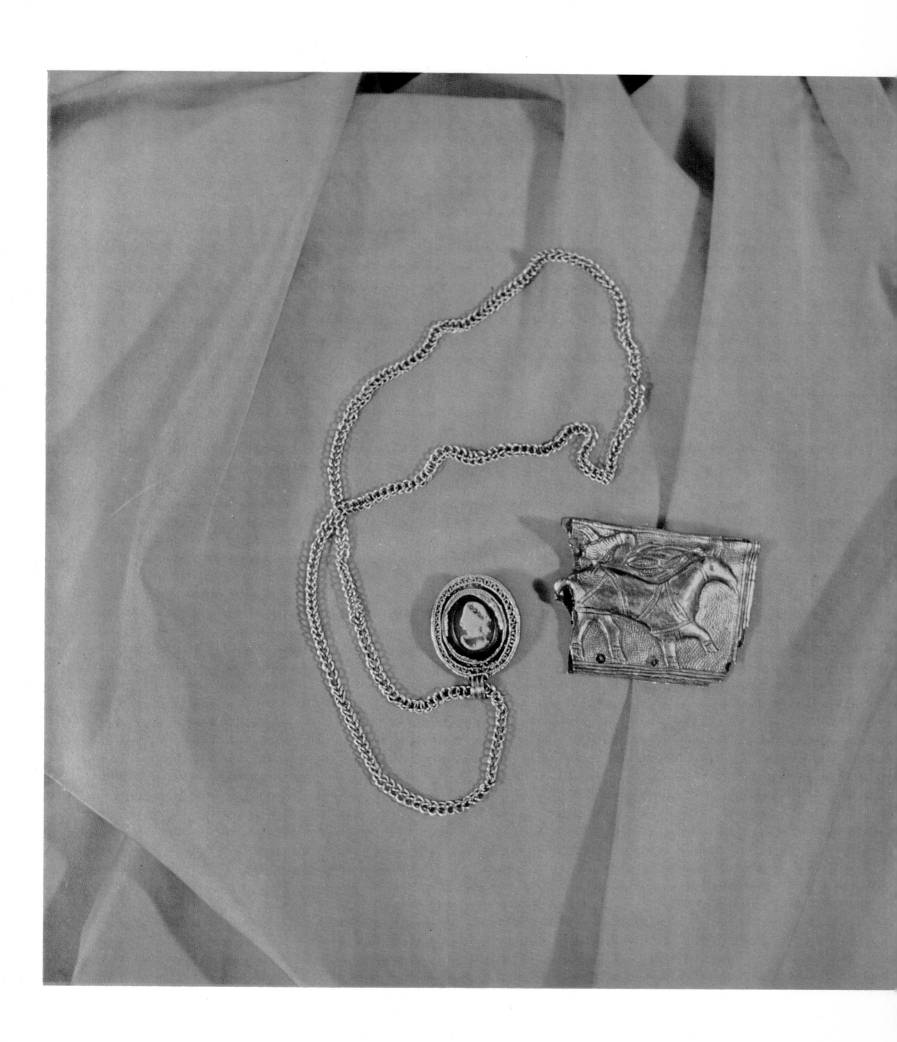

4   *Bronze Cup.* First half of 1st millennium B.C.
5   *Bronze Mask-like Brooch with Inlay on Bow.* 4th century B.C.
6   *Bronze Figure of Boar.* 1st century B.C.

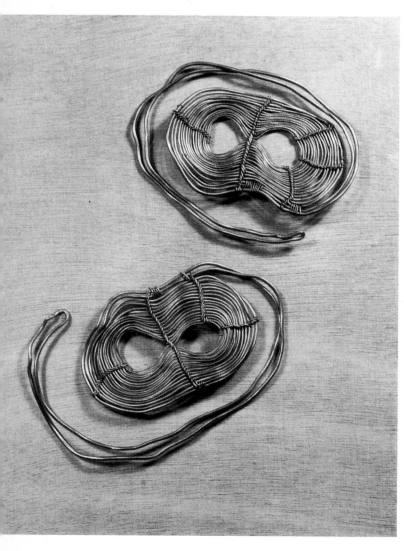

7 *Earthenware Sculpture of Bull.*
First half of 2nd millennium B.C.

8 *Two Eight-like Scrolls of Gold Wire.*
End of 2nd millennium B.C.

9 *Bronze Figure of Trumpeter (?).* 1st century B.C.

10 *Two Bronze Hatchets of Křtěnov Type.*
Beginning of second half of 2nd millennium B.C.

93

11 *Třeboň Antependium*. Bohemia. About 1380
12 *Pavese (Hussite War Shield)*. Kutná Hora. Mid-15th century

94

13 *Last Supper*. Bohemian Master. About 1500
14 *Guild Goblet of Goldsmiths of Prague Lesser Quarter*. 16th century

15 *Romanesque Coronet.* Bohemia. First half of 12th century
16 *Aquaemanale in Form of Fabulous Animal.* Hradec Králové, 12th century
17 *Romanesque Tile with Griffin.* Prague, Vyšehrad. 12th century

18 *Stove Tile with Equestrian Figure of Hussite War Leader*
   Jan Žižka of Trocnov. Prague. First half of 15th century
19a *Guild Flagon of United Guild of Bakers, Millers,*
   and Gingerbread Makers of Town of Slaný. Bohemia. 1577
19b *Detail of Engraving and Inscription*

20 *Glass Tankard*. Bohemia. 1579
21 *Book-shaped Bottle with Screw Cap*. Horní Slavkov. Second half of 17th century

24 *Sculpture. Tutelary Deity.* Red Indians. Northwest Coast, North America
25 *Uli Figure.* New Ireland. 19th century

26 *Head of Buddha*. India. 2nd to 3rd century
27 *Horse at Stake*. China. Colored inks on silk

28 *Figure-shaped Scraper*. Peru. Inca period
29 *Portrait of Buddhist Priest*. Japan. 16th century (?)

55   Master of Třeboň Altar. *Resurrection*. About 1380-1390
56   Pieter Brueghel the Elder. *The Haymakers*. About 1565

59   Paul Gauguin. *Bonjour, Monsieur Gauguin.* 1889
60   Pablo Picasso. *Self-portrait.* 1907

131

61   Václav Špála. *On the Otava before a Thunderstorm.* 1929

62   František Kupka. *Amorpha. Two-colored Fugue.* 1912

64   Albrecht Dürer. *Rosary Feast.* 1506

65 Henri Rousseau. *Self-portrait*. 1890
66 Bohemian master. *St. Nicholas of Rožmberk*. About 1380 to 1390

136

67   Domenico Theotocopuli (called El Greco). *Bust of Christ*. About 1590

68 Jan Gossaert (called Mabuse). *Madonna and St. Luke*. About 1513

139

69   Frans Hals the Elder. *Portrait of Jasper Schade van Westrum*. About 1645

70 Aert de Gelder (Arento de Geldera). *Vertumnus and Pomona*. Probably after 1685

71 Francisco José de Goya y Lucientes. *Portrait of Don Miguel de Lardizábal*. 1815
72 Paul Cézanne. *House at Aix*. Before 1885

73 Auguste Rodin. *St. John the Baptist.* 1878

75 Master of Vyšší Brod Altar. *The Lord's Nativity*. About 1350

76 Bohemian master. *Madonna of St. Vitus*. About 1400

79 Petr Jan Brandl. *Portrait of Man in White Wig*. About 1730

84 Mikoláš Aleš. *Žalov.* 1880
85 Josef Mánes. *Morning Song.* 1856
86 Jan Preisler. *Black Lake.* 1904

87 Otto Gutfreund. *Anxiety.* 1911
88 Jan Štursa. *Eve.* 1909

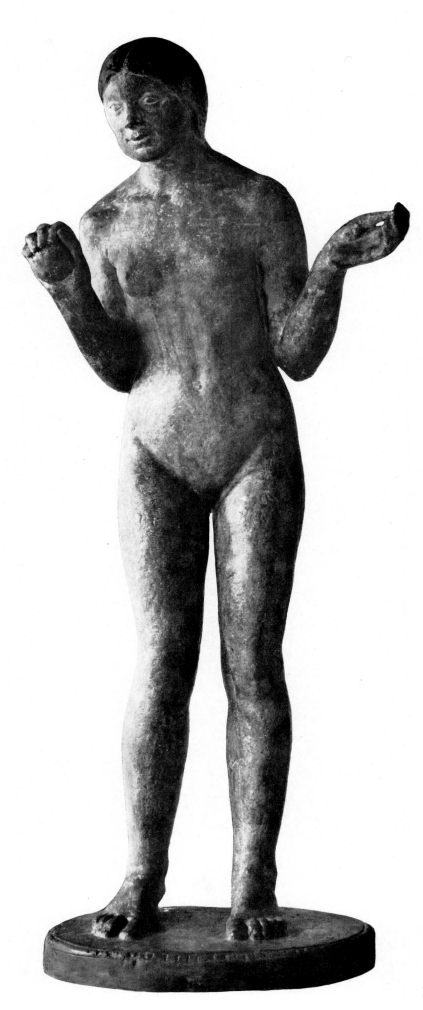

89 Bohumil Kubišta. *Old Prague Motif.* 1911
90 Josef Šíma. *Landscape.* 1930
91 Ludovít Fulla. *Expulsion from Paradise.* 1932

159

92 Bohemian master. *Madonna of Strakonice*. About 1325
93 Jan Zrzavý. *Sleeping Boats*. 1935

94   Rembrandt van Rijn. *Scholar at a Table* (also known as *The Rabbi*). 1634

MUSEUM OF DECORATIVE ART

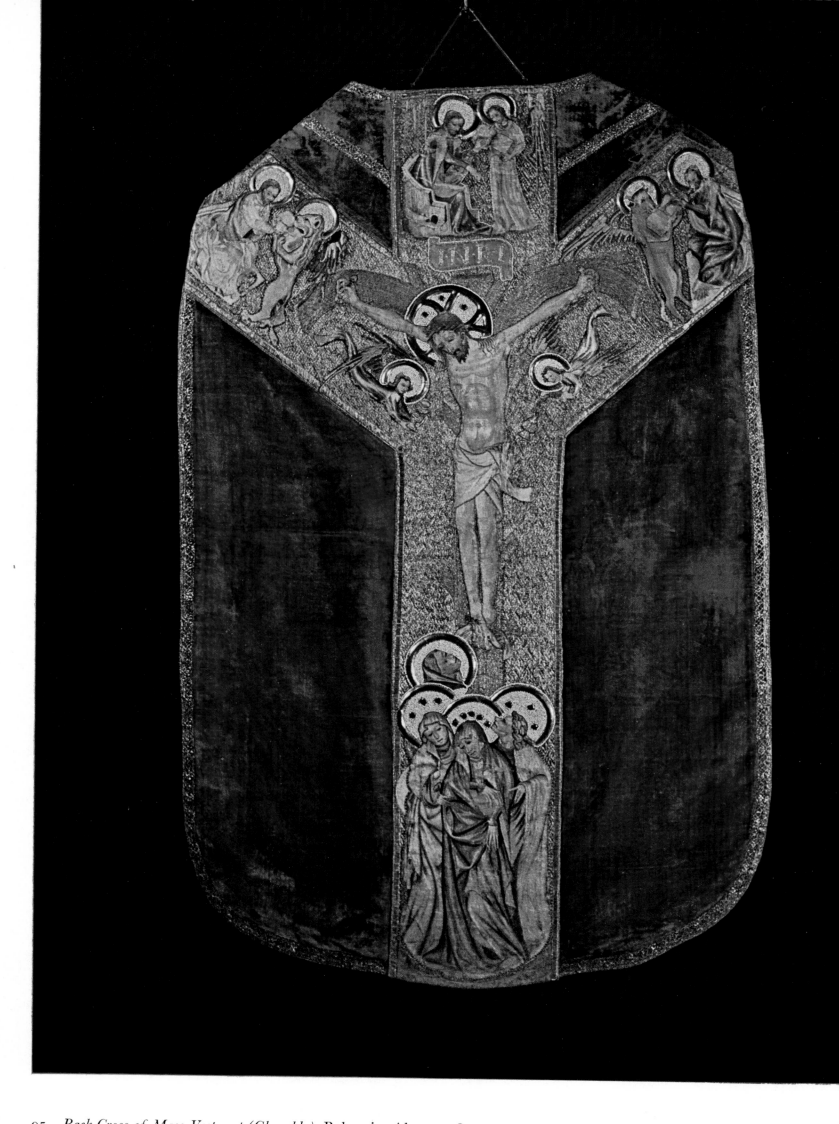

95 *Back Cross of Mass Vestment (Chasuble)*. Bohemia. About 1380

96 *Glass Sculpture*. Pavel Hlava. 1971
97 *Majolica Plate*. F. X. Avelli of Rovigo. 1540

98 *Beaker*. Cut by Kašpar Lehmann. Bohemia. 1605
99 a *Cabinet*. Prague. Third quarter of 17th century
99 b *Detail of Middle Part*

169

170

100   *Goblet with Lid*. Bohemia. Early 17th century
101   *Empire Vase*. Slavkov. 1840

104 *Hyacinth Princess*. Poster. Alfons Mucha. Prague. 1911

106 *Enamel Plate Showing Archangel Michael.* Byzantium. 12th century
107 *Lead Plaquette.* Paulus van Vianen. Prague. Beginning of 17th century
108 *Lead Plaquette.* Paulus van Vianen. Prague. Beginning of 17th century

MUSEUM OF THE CITY OF PRAGUE

112 *Man's Head*. From Relief in Bridge Tower of Charles Bridge in Lesser Quarter of Prague. About 1170   183

113   *Miniature Figurines*. Prague. 15th to 16th century
114   *Cup*. Prague. About 1400

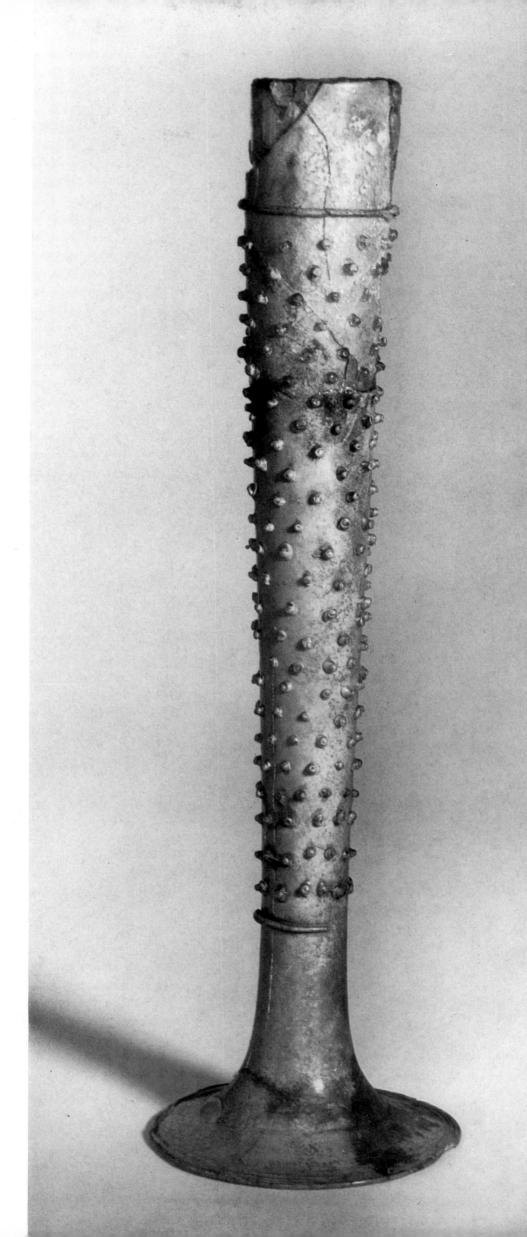

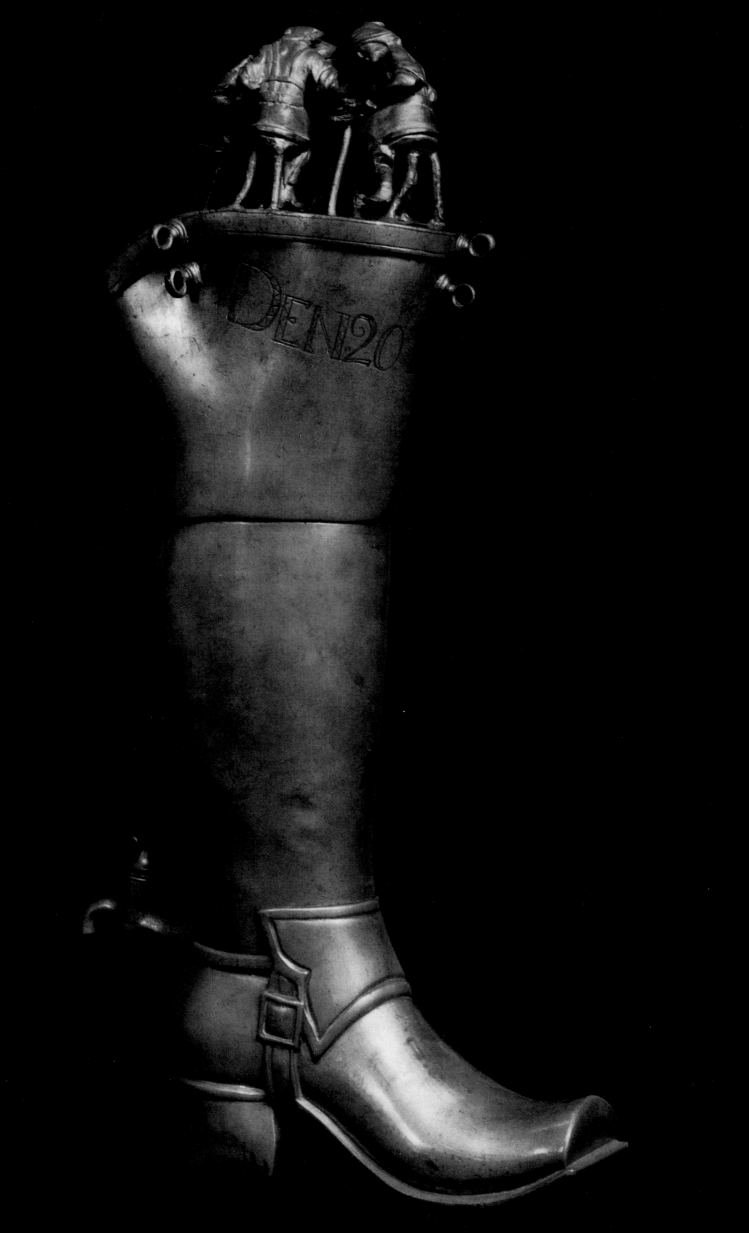

119 Bohemian master. *Head of John the Baptist*. About 1510-1520
120 Adriaen de Vries. *Hercules with Apples of Hesperides*. After 1620

TREASURY OF ST. VITUS' CATHEDRAL

125 *Coronation Jewels of Kingdom of Bohemia*
   a *Crown of St. Wenceslas*. Prague. 1346
   b *Apple*. Prague. Court workshop of Rudolph II. About 1605
   c *Scepter*. Prague. Court workshop of Rudolph II. About 1605

198

126 *Reliquary Cross of Pope Urban V.* Rome or Prague. About 1375
127 *Reliquary of St. Nicholas.* Venice. First half of 13th century

202

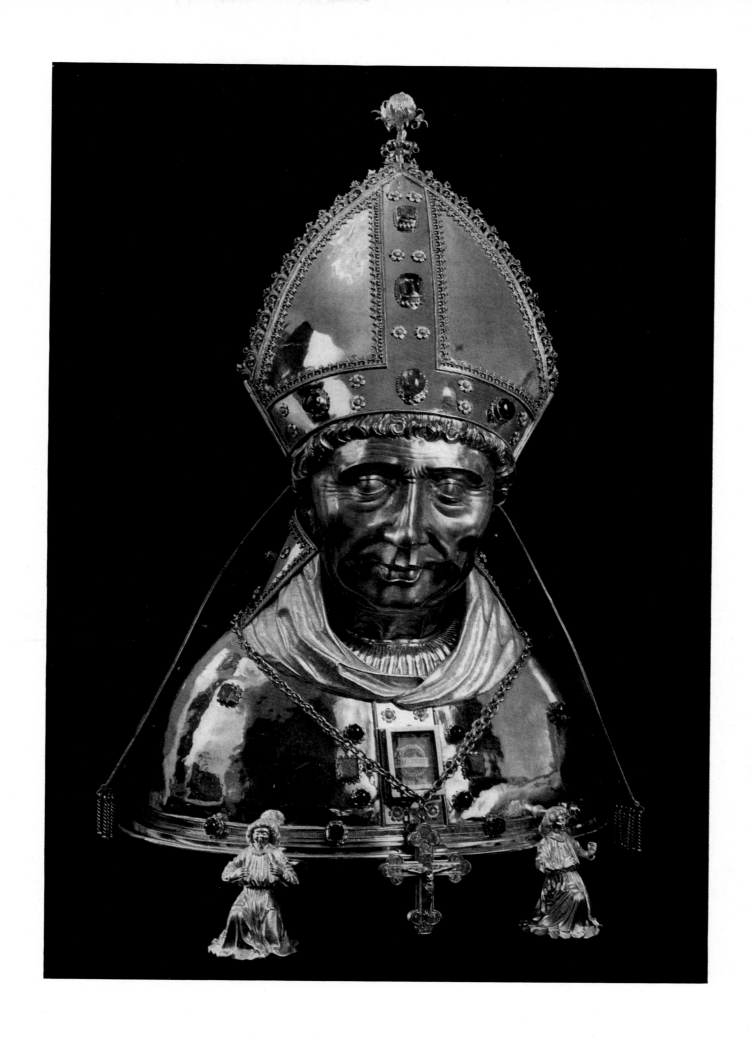

130 *Relic Can.* Prague. 1348. Lid: Prague. First half of 16th century
131 *Reliquary Bust of St. Vojtěch.* Prague. About 1486

132 *Ivory Horn (Olyphant)*. South Italy. 11th century

133 *Helmet of St. Wenceslas*. Western Europe. 9th century

134 *Pearl embroidery on cloth*. Prague.
Second half of 14th century

135   *Coronation Cross with Relics of Martyrdom of Christ.* France. 13th century

136   Paolo Caliari (called Veronese). *St. Catherine and the Angel*. Detail. About 1580
137   Paolo Caliari (called Veronese). *Christ Washing the Feet of His Disciples*. 1580's
138   Jacopo Robusti (called Tintoretto). *The Flagellation of Christ*. About 1555

139 Jacopo da Ponte (called Bassano). *The Good Samaritan*. After 1550
140 Domenico Fetti. *The Sower of Tares*. About 1621

141 Bartholomeus Spranger. *Allegory on Triumph of Loyalty over Fate.* 1607

214

142 Hans von Aachen. *Head of a Young Girl*. After 1610

143   Guido Reni. *The Centaur Nessus and Deianeira*. Before 1630

144   Peter Paul Rubens. *The Council of the Gods*. Probably 1602

145 Jan Kupecký. *Portrait of Jan Oldřich Sichart*. Between 1723 and 1726

146   Tiziano Vecellio (called Titian). *Portrait of a Young Woman at Her Toilet*. About 1520

147   Petr Brandl. *Paul the Apostle.* After 1725

STATE JEWISH MUSEUM

148 *Synagogue Curtain.* Turnov. About 1750

149 *Jug of Burial Brotherhood*. Brno. Dated 1720 and 1801
150 *Torah Decoration* (Plate). Prague. 1708

151 *Spice Container*. Brno. Mid-19th century
152 *Spice Container*. Austria. 1807-1813
153 *Spice Container*. Prague. End of 18th century

227

154 *Torah Pennon*. Loštice. 1750
155 *Levite Set*. Master J. J. Lux.
        Prague. 1702

156 *Book, Seder*. Prague.
    1514. Woodcut
157 *Pewter Set*. Bohemia.
    Mid-18th century

הָא לַחְמָא עַנְיָא דִי אֲ
כָלוּ אַבְהָתָנָא בְ
אַרְעָא דְמִצְרָיִם
כָּל דִכְפִין יֵיתֵי וְיֵכוֹל
כָּל דִצְרִיךְ יֵיתֵי
וְיִפְסַח הַשַּׁתָּא הָכָא
לְשָׁנָה הַבָּאָה בְּאַרְעָ

158 *Book, Haggada.* Prague. 1526. Woodcut   230

MILITARY MUSEUM

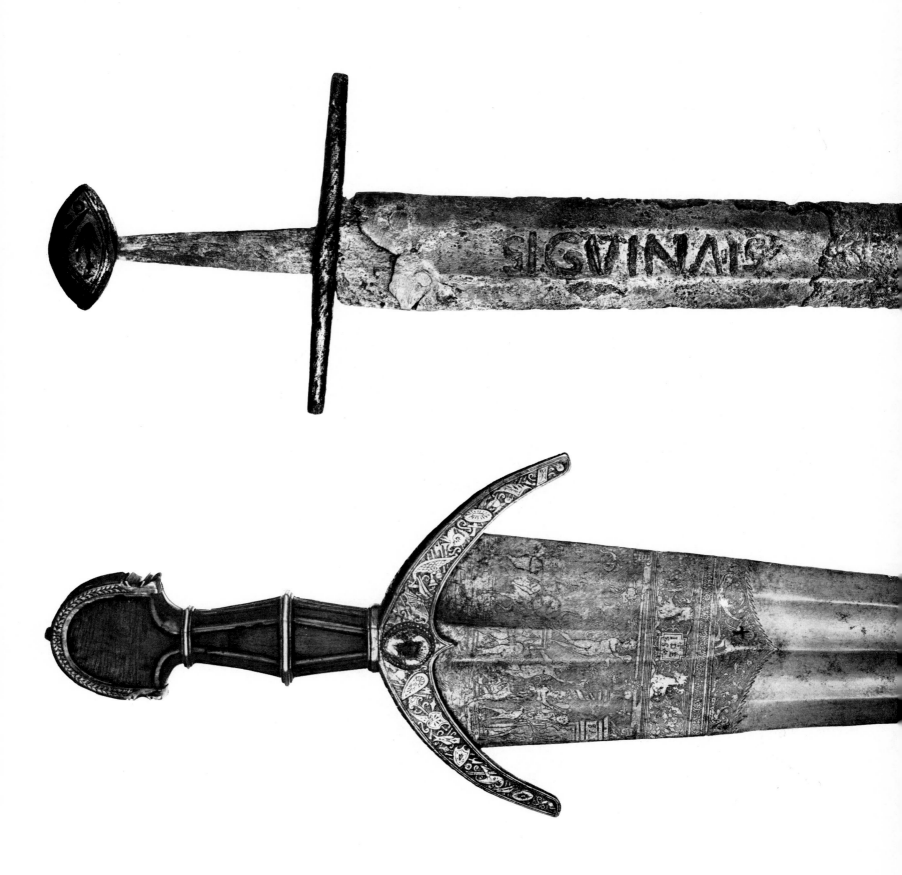

159   *Romanesque Sword*. Second half of 11th century
160   *Italian Dagger (Cinquedea)*. Workshop of Ercole dei Fideli. Ferrara. 1480-1500

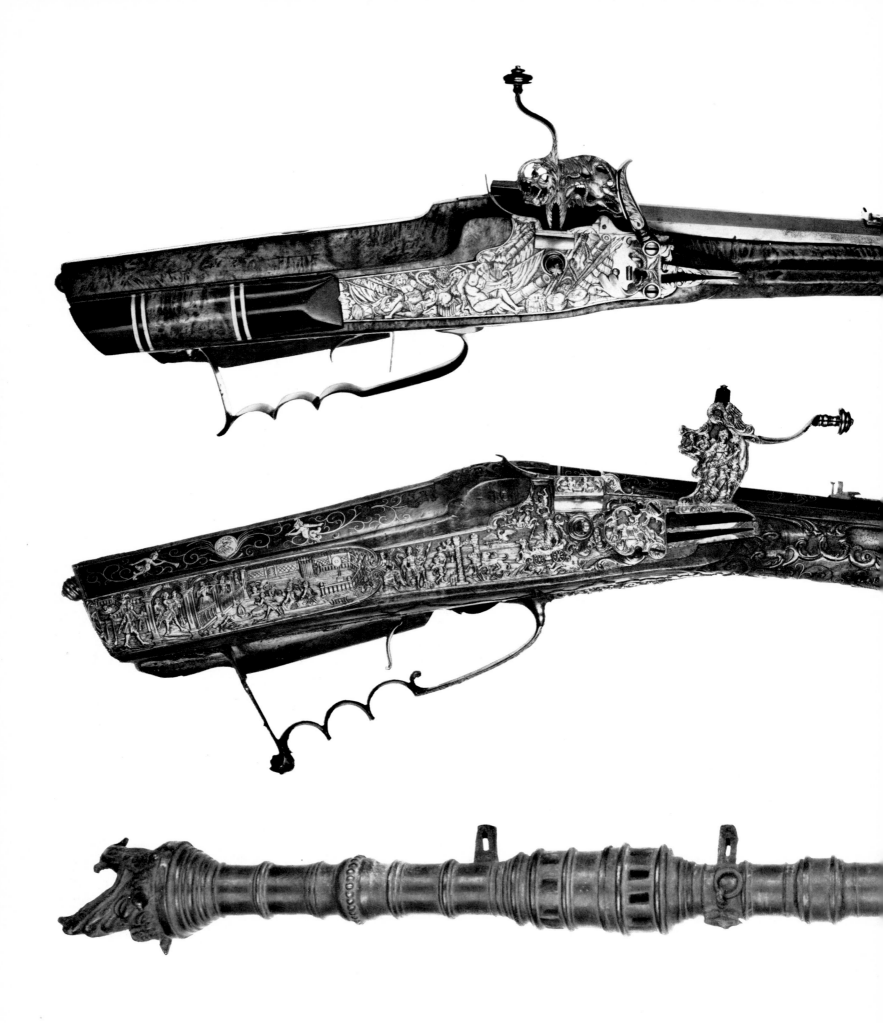

161 *Wheel-lock Rifle* (Detail). Georg A. Feiler. Karlovy Vary. End of 17th century

162 *Wheel-lock Rifle* (Detail). Leopold Becher the Elder. Karlovy Vary. About 1726-1728

163 *Bronze Barrel*. Northern Italy, Toscana (?). Last quarter of 15th century

234

164 *Pair of Stirrups*. Unknown master. Prague. Second half of 16th century

235

165   *Helmet (Pear-shaped Morion)*. Northern Italy. Third quarter of 16th century

ILLUMINATED MANUSCRIPTS
IN PRAGUE LIBRARIES

166 *Christ in Mandorla*. From *Codex Vyšehradensis*, Coronation Gospel Book.
About 1085. Prepared for coronation of Vratislav II

Pater quid nate gremio me confoue graue
In gremio matris residet sapiencia patris.
Tu michi nate pater et tu michi filia mater.

167 *Heavenly Jerusalem*. St. Augustine. From *De civitate Dei*. About 1200
168 *Madonna on Throne*. From *Codex Ostroviensis* (Psalter). About 1200

Eft ihc ablat? q. nescio quo tumulat? ┼ Surrexisse ihin monstrat uacuú monumentú;

169 *The Three Marys and Angel at Christ's Open Tomb*. From *Sedlec Antiphonary*. First half of 13th century
170 *Building of Tower of Babylon*. From illustrated bible called *Velislav Bible*. About 1340

Veñe iñt fecieñ9 nob cuitatē . ⁊ trim . cui9 culiñ pūtiñg ustz ad celū ⁊ celebrem9 nōm nrm āñ qͦ dñudeñ
deſteb auſe dñs uͭ uideͣ cuitatē . uͭ trm āñ ... edificabāt filꝯ noe ⁊ dixꝯ eͭc uñ9

Gen. 11. der Thurm   Babel.

popul9 ⁊ uium9 labiū oīb9 veſtc
lingiā eoꝛ uͭ nͦ andiaͭ

ſ deſtū dā ... nͦ ⁊ cͦfundā
... qͣ ſtz uoꝛm

Proxim9 ſui ⁊ ita eͦs diuiſio ⁊ tͦ nomẽ ⁊ nomẽ ci9
zBabel ⁊ ꝛfuſio

171 *Annunciation of Our Virgin.* Conradus de Haimburg. From *Laus Mariae.* Before 1364
172 *Stigmatization of St. Francis of Assisi.* From *Vitae* (Lives of the Fathers). 1516

245

Ihe saluta matrem sua cum osulo pacis dicens.

Salue mellita mea floscula vgo maria.

satbati aurea rutilacione resplenduit nixta
quod psalmigraphus longe antea phetauit
Nox inquiens sicut dies illuminabitur Et
sic facta est hec nox illuminacio mea fideli
te meis psam subito nuchi dilectus filius asti
tit et refulgente inhabitatulo lumine bys
uerbis me dulciter salutauit Aue inquit
mater nu aue Quasi dicat ve iam merous
depone quia sine ve me inutero concepisti et
sine dolous molestia uirgo pmanens peperisti
plangere desine lacrunas absterge gemitus re
pelle suspiria reice iam enim implete sut scrip
ture quia oportuit me pati et amortius resur
gere Iam prostrato pncipe mortis infernum
exspoliaui potestatem nicelo et terra accepi et
ouem perditam adouile pro humero repor
taui quia hominem qui perierat ad regna
celestia reuocaui Gaude igitur mater aman
tissima quia facta es celi et terre regina
Sc sicut morte interueniente obtinui dominiu
inferorum sic ascensionis gloria refulgente
regnu accipiam super noz Ascendam igitur
ad patrem meum ut preparem me diligen
tibus locum Tu autem surge dilecta mea co
lumba mea speciosa mea electa michi z pre
electa incipe iam npresenti gaudiu tibi nifu
turo longe glorious eternaliter pniasuz Ulti
mo sum montem syon matre cu discipulis con

173 *Christ's Mystic Embrace with Mary.* From *Passional of Abbess Kunhuta.* Prague. 1314-1321
174 *Annunciation of Our Virgin* From *Liber viaticus Joannis Noviforensis.* 1360-1364

175 *St. Jerome at Writing Stand.* From *Officium of St. Jerome*. Cheb. 1404
176 *Initial S with Kneeling King David.* From *Lobkovicz Breviary*. 1494

250

177 *Hussite Mass*. From *Codex of Jena*. About 1500
178 *John the Evangelist*. From *Gospel Book of St. Martin's Monastery* in Treves. End of 10th century

179   *Binding.* From *Gospel Book of St. Martin's Monastery* in Treves. 12th to 17th century

G A

M V L T A V